Juicing Recipes for Rapid Weight Loss

50 Delicious, Quick & Easy Recipes to Help Melt Your Damn Stubborn Fat Away!

Copyright © 2015 by Fat Loss Nation

All rights reserved. No part of this book may be reproduced in any form without permission in writing from the author. Reviewers are able to quote brief passages in reviews.

Disclaimer

This document is geared towards providing exact and reliable information in regards to the topic and issue covered. The publication is sold with the idea that the publisher is not required to render accounting, officially permitted, or otherwise, qualified services. If advice is necessary, legal or professional, a practiced individual in the profession should be ordered.

- From a Declaration of Principles which was accepted and approved equally by a Committee of the American Bar Association and a Committee of Publishers and Associations.

In no way is it legal to reproduce, duplicate, or transmit any part of this document in either electronic means or in printed format. Recording of this publication is strictly prohibited and any storage of this document is not allowed unless with written permission from the publisher. All rights reserved.

The information provided herein is stated to be truthful and consistent, in that any liability, in terms of inattention or otherwise, by any usage or abuse of any policies, processes, or directions contained within is the solitary and utter responsibility of the recipient reader. Under no circumstances will any legal responsibility or blame be held against the publisher for any reparation, damages, or monetary loss due to the information herein, either directly or indirectly.

Respective authors own all copyrights not held by the publisher.

The information herein is offered for informational purposes solely, and is universal as so. The presentation of the information is without contract or any type of guarantee assurance.

The trademarks that are used are without any consent, and the publication of the trademark is without permission or backing by the trademark owner. All trademarks and brands within this book are for clarifying purposes only and are the owned by the owners themselves, not affiliated with this document.

About This Book

This book aims to introduce you to the benefits of juicing and give you 50 of the best juice recipes for rapid weight loss. It's informational and to the point, and organized into sections on fruit juices, vegetable juices, and mixed juices so you won't be missing anything. Each section is complete with the needed information.

You will find concluding remarks and a list of resources for additional recipes at the end of this book. I will also give you a preview of another book of mine which I am sure will delight you as well.

The following table of contents will show you exactly what is covered in this book.

Table of Contents

Introduction 1

Tips for Juicing 3

Fruit Juice Recipes 5

   Apple Pear Lime 5

   Strawberry Blueberry Apple 8

   Kiwi Grape Peach 11

   Blackberry Grape 14

   Grapefruit Orange Lemon 17

   Blueberry Pomegranate 20

   Apple Pineapple Lime 23

   Pineapple Pomegranate Papaya 26

   Strawberry Blueberry Raspberry 29

   Kiwi Pear Apple 32

   Pineapple Cranberry Apple 35

   Apple Watermelon 38

   Strawberry Grape Orange 41

   Peach Apricot Grape 44

Vegie Juice Recipes 47

   Celery Cucumber Spinach 47

   Carrot Spinach Cucumber 48

   Celery Tomato Cabbage 49

   Turnip Carrot Watercress 50

   Broccoli Cabbage Kale 51

   Fresh Salsa 54

   V-7 Cocktail 57

Tomato Carrot Celery	60
Spinach Carrot	61
Beet Carrot	62
Cucumber Tomato	63
Spirulina Beet Spinach	64

Mixed Recipes 67

Spinach Splendor	67
Ginger Beet	70
Carrot Lemon Zest	73
Beets & Treats	76
Apple Melon Kale	79
Green Citrus	82
Pepper Carrot Apple	85
Tomato Strawberry Ginger	88
Cucumber Kiwi Mint	91
Spinach Ginger Lemon	94
Celery Citrus Cucumber Cocktail	97
Strawberry Pineapple Mint	100
Tropical Green	103
Apple Celery Ginger	106
Pineapple Broccoli Cucumber	109
Carrot Pineapple Chili	112
Ginger Pear Celery	115
Spicy Lemonade	118
Carrot Spinach Citrus	121
Mean Green	124

The Any Time Cocktail..127

Apple Cucumber Spinach 130

Celery Carrot Cucumber Cocktail...................................... 133

Red Tangy Spice.. 136

Conclusion 139

Helpful Resources 140

Preview of Gluten Free Diet Guide: A Blueprint to Jump Starting a Healthy, Low Budget, Gluten-Free Diet................. 141

Did You Like This Book? 144

More Books You Might Like... 145

Introduction

Does it frustrate you that so many diet recipe books don't provide you with basic information like the amount of calories and fat in a recipe? It frustrates me, which is why I'm including a complete nutritional analysis for every recipe in this book, *Juicing Recipes for Rapid Weight Loss*. This analysis will include vitamins, minerals, fat, sodium and everything else you need to make sure you're getting the nutrition you need without getting too much fat or too many calories.

Juicing is a terrific means of losing weight, because juicing provides you with most of the nutrients from the original food without most of the calories. And juicing also detoxifies your system, flushing away impurities, while at the same time supercharging you with extra vitamins, minerals, chlorophyll, antioxidants, enzymes and other beneficial ingredients. Juice provides you with the nutrients you need without a lot of fat, salt or sugar additives.

Juice also serves as a natural appetite suppressant to curb your calorie intake. Most commonly-used appetite suppressants contain additives that can prove harmful to one's health, but fresh-squeezed juice from your own juicer contains no additives. If you drink a glass of fresh juice a half hour before a meal, your appetite will noticeably diminish by mealtime.

Juicing has been demonstrated to help build health by:

1. Increasing weight loss

2. Lowering blood pressure

3. Containing cataracts

4. Preventing colon and breast cancer

5. Stabilizing blood pressure

6. Containing asthma

7. Preventing Alzheimer's

8. Protecting bones

9. Lowering cholesterol

10. Improving digestion

11. Strengthening the immune system

12. Preventing heart disease

13. Reducing inflammation

14. General cleansing of the body

This book provides a wide variety of recipes featuring numerous healthy foods, offering you many delicious ways to build all aspects of your health.

Thanks for downloading this book. I hope you enjoy it and find it useful.

Tips for Juicing

One of the most effective uses for juicing is as a replacement for a meal. While extended juice fasting for days at a time can occasionally provide a good cleansing, it can also lead to binging. Getting into the habit of replacing one meal a day with juice can provide a less drastic, more gradual cleansing without as much of a desire for binging.

Another great use for juice is as an appetite suppressant – drinking a glass of juice at least a half hour before a meal in order to partially satisfy your hunger. It's amazing how well this can work in helping to control the amount of food you eat. The nutrients provided by the juice help fool your body into thinking you've already eaten a meal, so your body starts shutting down your appetite.

It's best to drink juice on an empty stomach. Because juice is such a highly concentrated source of nutrition, it's a little more difficult to digest than many people think. Juice is so complex, concentrated and intense that it's a bit tough for your digestive system to handle and sort out.

Plus, you want the juice to flow through your system quickly, so that it can rapidly get to work flushing your system out. If you drink juice on a stomach that has food in it, the juice will get bogged down, sometimes for hours, and won't have a chance to flush your system out. Drinking juice on an empty stomach also enables the vitamins and minerals it provides to instantly go to work in your bloodstream.

As a general rule, finish drinking your juice at least twenty minutes before starting a meal, and wait until at least two hours after a meal before drinking juice.

Drink the juice immediately after you make it, because many enzymes and vitamins start to decay within minutes after coming out of the juicer. If you can't drink it all at once, refrigerate the portion you can't drink.

Fruit juices are a terrific pick-me-up and a good way to get your own juices flowing in the morning. Drinking fruit juice is a great idea just before exercising. But drinking more than one or two glasses of fruit juice can bring your sugar levels up too high, unless you're an avid exerciser. Drinking two or three glasses of mixed vegetable and fruit juice is a good way to give you a small boost of energy several times a day without raising your sugar levels quite as high.

If you like sweet drinks but are afraid of getting too much sugar, carrot juice is pretty darn sweet and can be mixed with a variety of other vegetables, providing sweetness without raising your sugar levels much, if at all.

Remember that juice is basically a food, so you have to "chew" it to mix it with your saliva. In other words, slosh it around in your mouth a little bit before you swallow it. People might wonder why you're gargling your juice, but maybe you'll start the latest fad.

Some juicers, after drinking their first smoothie, start to wonder whether they should switch over to smoothies instead of just juicing. But there's no reason why you can't enjoy both; in fact, they complement each other fairly well. You can use a smoothie to replace one meal a day and use juice as an appetite suppressor for the other two meals.

For the record, if you clean your juicer right after juicing, you'll save yourself a lot of scrubbing later.

Fruit Juice Recipes

Who doesn't enjoy fruit juice? There aren't many things in the world that taste better than fresh-squeezed fruit juice. And fruit juice offers a quick energy punch that's hard to beat as a pick-me-up. Fruit juice is also great as a cleanser, as well as being loaded with antioxidants that fight aging. In general, these might be the easiest juices to digest, particularly on an empty stomach.

Apple Pear Lime

Because pears are so sweet, the sourness of the lime complements them nicely.

Yields 1 glass.

Ingredients

- 3 apples
- 2 pears
- 1 lime

Directions

Wash the apples and pears thoroughly. Put them into a juicer.

EITHER

Peel and slice the lime, add the slices to the juicer, and process them together with the apples and pears.

OR

Squeeze the lime by hand and add its juice to that of the apples and pears after processing them separately.

Serve immediately.

Nutrition Facts (Juiced)

Calories 289	
Calories from Fat 9.83	

	% Daily Value *
Total Fat 1.09g	3.11%
Saturated Fat 0.172g	0.86%
Monounsaturated Fat 0.245g	
Polyunsaturated Fat 0.455g	
Cholesterol 0mg	
Sodium 7mg	0.47%
Potassium 746mg	15.87%
Total Carbohydrate 95.68g	73.6%
Dietary Fiber 2.6g	6.84%
Sugars 64.8g	
Protein 2.22g	
Vitamin A 15µg	1.67%
Vitamin C 41.9mg	46.56%
Calcium 61mg	6.1%
Iron 1.19mg	14.88%

* The Percent Daily Values are based on a 2,000 calorie diet, so your values may change depending on your calorie needs. The values here may not be 100% accurate because the recipes have not been professionally evaluated nor have they been evaluated by the U.S. FDA.

Vitamins

Choline 28.1mg	**5.11%**
Folate 33µg	**8.25%**
Niacin 0.843mg	**5.27%**
Riboflavin 0.174mg	**13.38%**
Thiamin 0.109mg	**9.08%**
Vitamin B-12 0µg	
Vitamin B-6 0.249mg	**19.15%**
Vitamin D 0IU	
Vitamin E 1.09mg	**7.27%**
Vitamin K 19.7µg	**16.42%**
Minerals	
Copper 0.338mg	**37.56%**
Magnesium 39mg	**9.29%**
Phosphorus 80mg	**11.43%**
Selenium 0.4µg	**0.73%**
Zinc 0.45mg	**4.09%**
Other	
Caffeine 0mg	
Theobromine 0mg	
Water 577.63g	

All nutrient values are calculated from the USDA nutrition database.

Strawberry Blueberry Apple

Any juice with berries is loaded with antioxidants.

Yields 1 glass.

Ingredients

- 5 strawberries
- 1 cup blueberries
- 1 apple, cored

Directions

1. Wash the fruit thoroughly.
2. Put all the ingredients into a juicer and process them.
3. Serve immediately.

Nutrition Facts (Juiced)

Calories 111
Calories from Fat 5.69

	% Daily Value *
Total Fat 0.63g	1.8%
Saturated Fat 0.068g	0.34%
Monounsaturated Fat 0.068g	
Polyunsaturated Fat 0.254g	
Cholesterol 0mg	
Sodium 3mg	0.2%
Potassium 254mg	5.4%

Total Carbohydrate 34.49g	**26.53%**
Dietary Fiber 0.9g	**2.37%**
Sugars 24.75g	
Protein 1.26g	
Vitamin A 7µg	**0.78%**
Vitamin C 30.3mg	**33.67%**
Calcium 18mg	**1.8%**
Iron 0.54mg	**6.75%**

* The Percent Daily Values are based on a 2,000 calorie diet, so your values may change depending on your calorie needs. The values here may not be 100% accurate because the recipes have not been professionally evaluated nor have they been evaluated by the U.S. FDA.

Vitamins	
Choline 11.9mg	**2.16%**
Folate 16µg	**4%**
Niacin 0.644mg	**4.03%**
Riboflavin 0.081mg	**6.23%**
Thiamin 0.066mg	**5.5%**
Vitamin B-12 0µg	
Vitamin B-6 0.118mg	**9.08%**
Vitamin D 0IU	
Vitamin E 0.89mg	**5.93%**
Vitamin K 23.3µg	**19.42%**
Minerals	
Copper 0.105mg	**11.67%**
Magnesium 16mg	**3.81%**

Phosphorus 32mg	**4.57%**
Selenium 0.2μg	**0.36%**
Zinc 0.25mg	**2.27%**

Other

Caffeine 0mg	
Theobromine 0mg	
Water 218.53g	

All nutrient values are calculated from the USDA nutrition database.

Kiwi Grape Peach

A nice combo with a bit of an exotic twist.

Yields one glass.

Ingredients

- 1 green apple, cored
- 1 peach, pitted
- 2 cups red grapes
- 2 kiwis

Directions

1. Wash the fruit thoroughly.
2. Put all the ingredients into a juicer and process them.
3. Serve immediately.

Nutrition Facts (Juiced)

Calories 193
Calories from Fat 14.16

	% Daily Value *
Total Fat 1.57g	4.49%
Saturated Fat 0.084g	0.42%
Monounsaturated Fat 0.125g	
Polyunsaturated Fat 0.433g	
Cholesterol 0mg	
Sodium 5mg	0.33%
Potassium 893mg	19%

Total Carbohydrate 59.32g	**45.63%**
Dietary Fiber 1.8g	**4.74%**
Sugars 30.73g	
Protein 3.41g	
Vitamin A 28µg	**3.11%**
Vitamin C 102.3mg	**113.67%**
Calcium 93mg	**9.3%**
Iron 1.04mg	**13%**

* The Percent Daily Values are based on a 2,000 calorie diet, so your values may change depending on your calorie needs. The values here may not be 100% accurate because the recipes have not been professionally evaluated nor have they been evaluated by the U.S. FDA.

Vitamins

Choline 18.3mg	**3.33%**
Folate 35µg	**8.75%**
Niacin 1.292mg	**8.08%**
Riboflavin 0.09mg	**6.92%**
Thiamin 0.073mg	**6.08%**
Vitamin B-12 0µg	
Vitamin B-6 0.139mg	**10.69%**
Vitamin D 0IU	
Vitamin E 2.41mg	**16.07%**
Vitamin K 44.5µg	**37.08%**

Minerals

Copper 0.381mg	**42.33%**
Magnesium 50mg	**11.9%**
Phosphorus 98mg	**14%**
Selenium 0.3µg	**0.55%**
Zinc 0.5mg	**4.55%**

Other

Caffeine 0mg	
Theobromine 0mg	
Water 388.77g	

All nutrient values are calculated from the USDA nutrition database.

Blackberry Grape

The tartness of the blackberries goes nicely with the sweetness of the red grapes.

Yields one glass.

Ingredients

- 1 cup fresh blackberries
- 2 cups fresh red grapes

Directions

1. Wash the fruit thoroughly. Remove stems.
2. Put all the ingredients into a juicer and process them.
3. Serve immediately.

Nutrition Facts (Juiced)

Calories 78
Calories from Fat 9.78

	% Daily Value *
Total Fat 1.09g	**3.11%**
Saturated Fat 0.014g	0.07%
Monounsaturated Fat 0.047g	
Polyunsaturated Fat 0.282g	
Cholesterol 0mg	
Sodium 2mg	0.13%
Potassium 419mg	8.91%
Total Carbohydrate 27.24g	20.95%

Dietary Fiber 1.5g	**3.95%**
Sugars 4.92g	
Protein 2.42g	
Vitamin A 15µg	**1.67%**
Vitamin C 21.2mg	**23.56%**
Calcium 76mg	**7.6%**
Iron 0.95mg	**11.88%**

* The Percent Daily Values are based on a 2,000 calorie diet, so your values may change depending on your calorie needs. The values here may not be 100% accurate because the recipes have not been professionally evaluated nor have they been evaluated by the U.S. FDA.

Vitamins

Choline 8.6mg	**1.56%**
Folate 28µg	**7%**
Niacin 0.651mg	**4.07%**
Riboflavin 0.026mg	**2%**
Thiamin 0.02mg	**1.67%**
Vitamin B-12 0µg	
Vitamin B-6 0.03mg	**2.31%**
Vitamin D 0IU	
Vitamin E 1.18mg	**7.87%**
Vitamin K 20µg	**16.67%**

Minerals

Copper 0.316mg	**35.11%**
Magnesium 38mg	**9.05%**
Phosphorus 52mg	**7.43%**
Selenium 0.4µg	**0.73%**
Zinc 0.67mg	**6.09%**

Other

Caffeine 0mg
Theobromine 0mg
Water 195.06g

All nutrient values are calculated from the USDA nutrition database.

Grapefruit Orange Lemon

This citrus trio is packed with Vitamin C.

Yields one glass.

Ingredients

- 1 pink grapefruit
- 1 orange
- ½ lemon

Directions

1. Remove peels.
2. Squeeze by hand, in a citrus juicer or in a regular juicer.
3. Serve immediately.

Nutrition Facts (Juiced)

Calories 91
Calories from Fat 3.4

	% Daily Value *
Total Fat 0.38g	**1.09%**
Saturated Fat 0.05g	**0.25%**
Monounsaturated Fat 0.048g	
Polyunsaturated Fat 0.092g	
Cholesterol 0mg	
Sodium 1mg	**0.07%**
Potassium 456mg	**9.7%**
Total Carbohydrate 27.99g	**21.53%**

Dietary Fiber 0.7g	**1.84%**
Sugars 21.82g	
Protein 2.31g	
Vitamin A 93µg	**10.33%**
Vitamin C 126mg	**140%**
Calcium 66mg	**6.6%**
Iron 0.43mg	**5.38%**

* The Percent Daily Values are based on a 2,000 calorie diet, so your values may change depending on your calorie needs. The values here may not be 100% accurate because the recipes have not been professionally evaluated nor have they been evaluated by the U.S. FDA.

Vitamins

Choline 23mg	**4.18%**
Folate 49µg	**12.25%**
Niacin 0.736mg	**4.6%**
Riboflavin 0.078mg	**6%**
Thiamin 0.156mg	**13%**
Vitamin B-12 0µg	
Vitamin B-6 0.154mg	**11.85%**
Vitamin D 0IU	
Vitamin E 0.44mg	**2.93%**
Vitamin K 0µg	

Minerals

Copper 0.136mg	**15.11%**
Magnesium 26mg	**6.19%**
Phosphorus 32mg	**4.57%**
Selenium 1.1µg	**2%**
Zinc 0.21mg	**1.91%**

Other

Caffeine 0mg
Theobromine 0mg
Water 268.58g

All nutrient values are calculated from the USDA nutrition database.

Blueberry Pomegranate

Blueberries and pomegranate are two superstars in providing antioxidants.

Yields one glass.

Ingredients

- 1 cup pomegranate seeds
- 2 cups blueberries
- Sparkling water (pour into glass of finished juice)

Directions

1. Wash the fruit thoroughly.
2. Put the pomegranate seeds and blueberries into a juicer and process them.
3. Add sparkling water to taste.
4. Serve immediately.

Nutrition Facts (Juiced)

Calories 184
Calories from Fat 18.98

	% Daily Value *
Total Fat 2.11g	**6.03%**
Saturated Fat 0.204g	**1.02%**
Monounsaturated Fat 0.211g	
Polyunsaturated Fat 0.399g	
Cholesterol 0mg	

Sodium 6mg	0.4%
Potassium 447mg	9.51%
Total Carbohydrate 52.8g	40.62%
Dietary Fiber 1.4g	3.68%
Sugars 37.29g	
Protein 3.57g	
Vitamin A 6µg	0.67%
Vitamin C 32.5mg	36.11%
Calcium 25mg	2.5%
Iron 0.95mg	11.88%

* The Percent Daily Values are based on a 2,000 calorie diet, so your values may change depending on your calorie needs. The values here may not be 100% accurate because the recipes have not been professionally evaluated nor have they been evaluated by the U.S. FDA.

Vitamins	
Choline 21.7mg	3.95%
Folate 59µg	14.75%
Niacin 1.223mg	7.64%
Riboflavin 0.15mg	11.54%
Thiamin 0.158mg	13.17%
Vitamin B-12 0µg	
Vitamin B-6 0.199mg	15.31%
Vitamin D 0IU	
Vitamin E 1.91mg	12.73%
Vitamin K 60µg	50%
Minerals	

Copper 0.311mg	**34.56%**
Magnesium 27mg	**6.43%**
Phosphorus 69mg	**9.86%**
Selenium 0.8µg	**1.45%**
Zinc 0.76mg	**6.91%**

Other

Caffeine 0mg	
Theobromine 0mg	
Water 269.4g	

All nutrient values are calculated from the USDA nutrition database.

Apple Pineapple Lime

Pineapple juice is good for digestion and your kidneys.

Yields 1 glass.

Ingredients

- 3 apples, cored
- ½ pineapple
- ½ lime, peeled

Directions

1. Wash the fruit thoroughly.
2. Put all the ingredients into a juicer and process them.
3. Serve immediately.

Nutrition Facts (Juiced)

Calories 313
Calories from Fat 9.69

	% Daily Value *
Total Fat 1.08g	**3.09%**
Saturated Fat 0.141g	0.7%
Monounsaturated Fat 0.072g	
Polyunsaturated Fat 0.335g	
Cholesterol 0mg	
Sodium 7mg	0.47%
Potassium 778mg	16.55%
Total Carbohydrate 96.81g	74.47%

Dietary Fiber 2g	5.26%
Sugars 71.31g	
Protein 2.87g	
Vitamin A 21µg	2.33%
Vitamin C 175.8mg	195.33%
Calcium 72mg	7.2%
Iron 1.52mg	19%

* The Percent Daily Values are based on a 2,000 calorie diet, so your values may change depending on your calorie needs. The values here may not be 100% accurate because the recipes have not been professionally evaluated nor have they been evaluated by the U.S. FDA.

Vitamins

Choline 31.6mg	5.75%
Folate 70µg	17.5%
Niacin 1.978mg	12.36%
Riboflavin 0.205mg	15.77%
Thiamin 0.322mg	26.83%
Vitamin B-12 0µg	
Vitamin B-6 0.522mg	40.15%
Vitamin D 0IU	
Vitamin E 0.8mg	5.33%
Vitamin K 10.8µg	9%

Minerals

Copper 0.467mg	**51.89%**
Magnesium 59mg	**14.05%**
Phosphorus 72mg	**10.29%**
Selenium 0.4µg	**0.73%**
Zinc 0.56mg	**5.09%**

Other

Caffeine 0mg	
Theobromine 0mg	
Water 620.11g	

All nutrient values are calculated from the USDA nutrition database.

Pineapple Pomegranate Papaya

A touch of the tropics.

Yields 1 glass.

Ingredients

- 1 pineapple wedge, 1 inch thick
- Seeds of 1 pomegranate
- 1 small papaya
- 1 small nectarine

Directions

1. Wash the fruit thoroughly. Remove peels, pits and stems.
2. Put all the ingredients into a juicer and process them.
3. Serve immediately.

Nutrition Facts (Juiced)

Calories 266
Calories from Fat 27.48

	% Daily Value *
Total Fat 3.05g	8.71%
Saturated Fat 0.361g	1.81%
Monounsaturated Fat 0.365g	
Polyunsaturated Fat 0.378g	
Cholesterol 0mg	
Sodium 16mg	1.07%

Potassium 992mg	**21.11%**
Total Carbohydrate 74.54g	**57.34%**
Dietary Fiber 1.9g	**5%**
Sugars 54.87g	
Protein 5.49g	
Vitamin A 72µg	**8%**
Vitamin C 148mg	**164.44%**
Calcium 63mg	**6.3%**
Iron 1.48mg	**18.5%**

* The Percent Daily Values are based on a 2,000 calorie diet, so your values may change depending on your calorie needs. The values here may not be 100% accurate because the recipes have not been professionally evaluated nor have they been evaluated by the U.S. FDA.

Vitamins

Choline 34.3mg	**6.24%**
Folate 142µg	**35.5%**
Niacin 2.67mg	**16.69%**
Riboflavin 0.198mg	**15.23%**
Thiamin 0.283mg	**23.58%**
Vitamin B-12 0µg	
Vitamin B-6 0.345mg	**26.54%**
Vitamin D 0IU	
Vitamin E 2.3mg	**15.33%**
Vitamin K 38.2µg	**31.83%**

Minerals

Copper 0.575mg	**63.89%**
Magnesium 70mg	**16.67%**
Phosphorus 117mg	**16.71%**
Selenium 1.8µg	**3.27%**
Zinc 1.09mg	**9.91%**

Other

Caffeine 0mg
Theobromine 0mg
Water 437.61g

All nutrient values are calculated from the USDA nutrition database.

Strawberry Blueberry Raspberry

I think you can imagine how good this tastes.

Yields 1 glass.

Ingredients

- 2 cups strawberries
- 2 cups blueberries
- 1 ½ cups raspberries
- 1 apple, cored

Directions

1. Wash the fruit thoroughly.
2. Put all the ingredients into a juicer and process them.
3. Serve immediately.

Nutrition Facts (Juiced)

	% Daily Value *
Calories 242	
Calories from Fat 21.1	
Total Fat 2.34g	**6.69%**
Saturated Fat 0.148g	**0.74%**
Monounsaturated Fat 0.276g	
Polyunsaturated Fat 1.164g	
Cholesterol 0mg	
Sodium 7mg	**0.47%**
Potassium 799mg	**17%**

Total Carbohydrate 78.52g	**60.4%**
Dietary Fiber 2.9g	7.63%
Sugars 49.44g	
Protein 4.77g	
Vitamin A 15µg	1.67%
Vitamin C 178.3mg	198.11%
Calcium 85mg	8.5%
Iron 2.45mg	30.63%

* The Percent Daily Values are based on a 2,000 calorie diet, so your values may change depending on your calorie needs. The values here may not be 100% accurate because the recipes have not been professionally evaluated nor have they been evaluated by the U.S. FDA.

Vitamins

Choline 44.1mg	8.02%
Folate 92µg	23%
Niacin 2.533mg	15.83%
Riboflavin 0.212mg	16.31%
Thiamin 0.188mg	15.67%
Vitamin B-12 0µg	
Vitamin B-6 0.326mg	25.08%
Vitamin D 0IU	
Vitamin E 3.12mg	20.8%
Vitamin K 57.3µg	47.75%

Minerals

Copper 0.366mg	**40.67%**
Magnesium 73mg	**17.38%**
Phosphorus 125mg	**17.86%**
Selenium 1.3µg	**2.36%**
Zinc 1.21mg	**11%**

Other

Caffeine 0mg
Theobromine 0mg
Water 577.59g

All nutrient values are calculated from the USDA nutrition database.

Kiwi Pear Apple

Earthy green color. You can peel the kiwi if you want.

Yields 1 glass.

Ingredients

- 2 kiwis
- 3 pears, cored
- 1 apple, cored

Directions

1. Wash the fruit thoroughly.
2. Put all the ingredients into a juicer and process them.
3. Serve immediately.

Nutrition Facts (Juiced)

Calories 275
Calories from Fat 11.18

	% Daily Value *
Total Fat 1.24g	3.54%
Saturated Fat 0.146g	0.73%
Monounsaturated Fat 0.368g	
Polyunsaturated Fat 0.694g	
Cholesterol 0mg	
Sodium 8mg	0.53%
Potassium 871mg	18.53%
Total Carbohydrate 88.69g	68.22%

Dietary Fiber 2.5g	**6.58%**
Sugars 58.37g	
Protein 2.78g	
Vitamin A 11µg	1.22%
Vitamin C 111.5mg	123.89%
Calcium 74mg	7.4%
Iron 1.13mg	14.12%

* The Percent Daily Values are based on a 2,000 calorie diet, so your values may change depending on your calorie needs. The values here may not be 100% accurate because the recipes have not been professionally evaluated nor have they been evaluated by the U.S. FDA.

Vitamins

Choline 30.9mg	**5.62%**
Folate 54µg	**13.5%**
Niacin 1.047mg	**6.54%**
Riboflavin 0.154mg	**11.85%**
Thiamin 0.093mg	**7.75%**
Vitamin B-12 0µg	
Vitamin B-6 0.221mg	**17%**
Vitamin D 0IU	
Vitamin E 2.09mg	**13.93%**
Vitamin K 58.2µg	**48.5%**

Minerals

Copper 0.466mg	**51.78%**
Magnesium 49mg	**11.67%**
Phosphorus 92mg	**13.14%**
Selenium 0.6µg	**1.09%**
Zinc 0.56mg	**5.09%**

Other

Caffeine 0mg	
Theobromine 0mg	
Water 503.09g	

All nutrient values are calculated from the USDA nutrition database.

Pineapple Cranberry Apple

A tangy-sweet flavor.

Yields 1 glass.

Ingredients

- ½ pineapple
- ½ cup cranberries
- 1 apple, cored

Directions

1. Wash the fruit thoroughly.
2. Put all the ingredients into a juicer and process them.
3. Serve immediately.

Nutrition Facts (Juiced)

Calories 208
Calories from Fat 5.78

	% Daily Value *
Total Fat 0.64g	**1.83%**
Saturated Fat 0.068g	0.34%
Monounsaturated Fat 0.056g	
Polyunsaturated Fat 0.211g	
Cholesterol 0mg	
Sodium 5mg	0.33%
Potassium 511mg	10.87%
Total Carbohydrate 63.42g	**48.78%**

Dietary Fiber 1.3g	**3.42%**
Sugars 45.85g	
Protein 2.18g	
Vitamin A 14μg	**1.56%**
Vitamin C 161.9mg	**179.89%**
Calcium 52mg	**5.2%**
Iron 1.16mg	**14.5%**

* The Percent Daily Values are based on a 2,000 calorie diet, so your values may change depending on your calorie needs. The values here may not be 100% accurate because the recipes have not been professionally evaluated nor have they been evaluated by the U.S. FDA.

Vitamins

Choline 23.7mg	**4.31%**
Folate 61μg	**15.25%**
Niacin 1.735mg	**10.84%**
Riboflavin 0.141mg	**10.85%**
Thiamin 0.276mg	**23%**
Vitamin B-12 0μg	
Vitamin B-6 0.427mg	**32.85%**
Vitamin D 0IU	
Vitamin E 0.71mg	**4.73%**
Vitamin K 6.8μg	**5.67%**

Minerals

Copper 0.404mg	**44.89%**
Magnesium 46mg	**10.95%**
Phosphorus 44mg	**6.29%**
Selenium 0.4μg	**0.73%**
Zinc 0.47mg	**4.27%**

Other

Caffeine 0mg
Theobromine 0mg
Water 411.9g

All nutrient values are calculated from the USDA nutrition database.

Apple Watermelon

This has a sweet and light taste.

Yields 1 glass.

Ingredients

- 2 apples, cored
- 3 slices watermelon

Directions

1. Wash the fruit thoroughly.
2. Put all the ingredients into a juicer and process them.
3. Serve immediately.

Nutrition Facts (Juiced)

Calories 225
Calories from Fat 9.3

	% Daily Value *
Total Fat 1.03g	2.94%
Saturated Fat 0.135g	0.68%
Monounsaturated Fat 0.166g	
Polyunsaturated Fat 0.33g	
Cholesterol 0mg	
Sodium 7mg	0.47%
Potassium 721mg	15.34%
Total Carbohydrate 65.42g	50.32%
Dietary Fiber 1.1g	2.89%

Sugars 51.3g

Protein 3.1g

Vitamin A 120μg	**13.33%**
Vitamin C 44.2mg	**49.11%**
Calcium 43mg	**4.3%**
Iron 1.27mg	**15.88%**

* The Percent Daily Values are based on a 2,000 calorie diet, so your values may change depending on your calorie needs. The values here may not be 100% accurate because the recipes have not been professionally evaluated nor have they been evaluated by the U.S. FDA.

Vitamins

Choline 25.1mg	**4.56%**
Folate 20μg	**5%**
Niacin 0.945mg	**5.91%**
Riboflavin 0.15mg	**11.54%**
Thiamin 0.175mg	**14.58%**
Vitamin B-12 0μg	
Vitamin B-6 0.285mg	**21.92%**
Vitamin D 0IU	
Vitamin E 0.66mg	**4.4%**
Vitamin K 6μg	**5%**

Minerals

Copper 0.237mg	**26.33%**
Magnesium 53mg	**12.62%**
Phosphorus 72mg	**10.29%**
Selenium 1.6µg	**2.91%**
Zinc 0.5mg	**4.55%**

Other

Caffeine 0mg	
Theobromine 0mg	
Water 584.17g	

All nutrient values are calculated from the USDA nutrition database.

Strawberry Grape Orange

Flavorful and interesting.

Yields 1 glass.

Ingredients

- 1 cup strawberries
- 1 cup red grapes
- 1 orange, peeled

Directions

1. Wash the fruit thoroughly.
2. Put all the ingredients into a juicer and process them.
3. Serve immediately.

Nutrition Facts (Juiced)

Calories 87
Calories from Fat 6.38

	% Daily Value *
Total Fat 0.71g	**2.03%**
Saturated Fat 0.029g	0.15%
Monounsaturated Fat 0.064g	
Polyunsaturated Fat 0.179g	
Cholesterol 0mg	
Sodium 2mg	0.13%
Potassium 448mg	9.53%
Total Carbohydrate 27.29g	**20.99%**

Dietary Fiber 1g	**2.63%**
Sugars 13.5g	
Protein 2.05g	
Vitamin A 13µg	**1.44%**
Vitamin C 108.1mg	**120.11%**
Calcium 76mg	**7.6%**
Iron 0.67mg	**8.38%**

* The Percent Daily Values are based on a 2,000 calorie diet, so your values may change depending on your calorie needs. The values here may not be 100% accurate because the recipes have not been professionally evaluated nor have they been evaluated by the U.S. FDA.

Vitamins

Choline 13.4mg	**2.44%**
Folate 53µg	**13.25%**
Niacin 0.648mg	**4.05%**
Riboflavin 0.059mg	**4.54%**
Thiamin 0.104mg	**8.67%**
Vitamin B-12 0µg	
Vitamin B-6 0.102mg	**7.85%**
Vitamin D 0IU	
Vitamin E 0.46mg	**3.07%**
Vitamin K 2.2µg	**1.83%**

Minerals

Copper 0.165mg	**18.33%**
Magnesium 31mg	**7.38%**
Phosphorus 52mg	**7.43%**
Selenium 0.9μg	**1.64%**
Zinc 0.27mg	**2.45%**

Other

Caffeine 0mg	
Theobromine 0mg	
Water 224.33g	

All nutrient values are calculated from the USDA nutrition database.

Peach Apricot Grape

This is quite sweet and a little mushy. Nice for dessert.

Yields 1 glass.

Ingredients

- 2 peaches, pitted
- 2 apricots, pitted
- ½ cup green grapes

Directions

1. Wash the fruit thoroughly.
2. Put all the ingredients into a juicer and process them.
3. Serve immediately.

Nutrition Facts (Juiced)

Calories 104
Calories from Fat 7.78

	% Daily Value *
Total Fat 0.86g	2.46%
Saturated Fat 0	
Monounsaturated Fat 0	
Polyunsaturated Fat 0	
Cholesterol 0	
Sodium 1mg	0.07%
Potassium 590mg	12.55%
Total Carbohydrate 29.87g	22.98%

Dietary Fiber 0.8g	**2.11%**
Sugars 22	
Protein 2.85g	
Vitamin A 82μg	**9.11%**
Vitamin C 19	**21.11%**
Calcium 31mg	**3.1%**
Iron 0.8mg	**10%**

* The Percent Daily Values are based on a 2,000 calorie diet, so your values may change depending on your calorie needs. The values here may not be 100% accurate because the recipes have not been professionally evaluated nor have they been evaluated by the U.S. FDA.

Vitamins

Choline 14	**2.55%**
Folate 13μg	**3.25%**
Niacin 2	**12.5%**
Riboflavin 0	
Thiamin 0	
Vitamin B-12 0	
Vitamin B-6 0	
Vitamin D 0	
Vitamin E 2	**13.33%**
Vitamin K 7	**5.83%**

Minerals

Copper 0.219mg	**24.33%**
Magnesium 28mg	**6.67%**
Phosphorus 61mg	**8.71%**
Selenium 0	
Zinc 0.49mg	**4.45%**

Other

Caffeine 0	
Theobromine 0	
Water 255.49g	

All nutrient values are calculated from the USDA nutrition database.

Vegie Juice Recipes

Vegetable juices are absolutely packed with vitamins, nutrients, chlorophyll and other goodies. The combinations available are nearly endless, as vegetables combine so well with each other, not just on your taste buds but in your stomach acids as well, making them easier to digest that some fruit combinations. Because vegetable juice contains little sugar, it can help stabilize your blood sugar levels.

Celery Cucumber Spinach

Spinach is just packed with vitamins and minerals. Popeye was pretty smart.

Yields 1 glass.

Ingredients

- 1 medium cucumber
- 3 stalks of celery
- 3 to 4 handfuls of spinach

Directions

1. Wash the vegetables thoroughly.

2. Put all the ingredients into a juicer and process them. Best order is spinach first, celery second, cucumber third.

3. Ready to serve immediately.

Carrot Spinach Cucumber

Straight carrot juice is a bit sweet for some people, so mixing it with cucumber and spinach dials the sweetness down.

Yields 1 glass.

Ingredients

- 4 medium carrots
- 3 handfuls spinach
- 1 medium cucumber

Directions

1. Wash the vegetables thoroughly.
2. Put all the ingredients into a juicer and process them.
3. Serve immediately.

Celery Tomato Cabbage

A nice, mellow combination. Tomato juice is a favorite worldwide.

Yields 1 glass.

Ingredients

- ½ cabbage
- 3 stalks celery
- ½ tomato
- 2 carrots

Directions

1. Wash the vegetables thoroughly. Cut the tops off the carrots.

2. Put all the ingredients into a juicer and process them.

3. Serve immediately.

Turnip Carrot Watercress

This is a good blood builder with quite a bit of chlorophyll. Unusual flavor.

Yields 1 glass.

Ingredients

- 5 carrots
- 8 spinach leaves
- 5 turnip leaves
- 5 sprigs watercress

Directions

1. Wash the vegetables thoroughly.
2. Put all the ingredients into a juicer and process them.
3. Serve immediately.

Broccoli Cabbage Kale

A trio of cabbage family vegies, making this recipe among the easiest to digest.

Yields 1 glass.

Ingredients

- 1 stalk broccoli
- ½ head cabbage
- 4 leaves kale

Directions

1. Wash the vegetables thoroughly.
2. Put all the ingredients into a juicer and process them.
3. Serve immediately.

Nutrition Facts (Juiced)

Calories 125
Calories from Fat 14.58

	% Daily Value *
Total Fat 1.62g	4.63%
Saturated Fat 0.238g	1.19%
Monounsaturated Fat 0.117g	
Polyunsaturated Fat 0.425g	
Cholesterol 0mg	
Sodium 129mg	8.60%
Potassium 1355mg	28.83%

Total Carbohydrate 34.03g	**26.18%**
Dietary Fiber 2	**5.26%**
Sugars 12	
Protein 11.24g	
Vitamin A 539µg	**59.89%**
Vitamin C 328.2mg	**364.67%**
Calcium 324mg	**32.40%**
Iron 3.71mg	**46.38%**

* The Percent Daily Values are based on a 2,000 calorie diet, so your values may change depending on your calorie needs. The values here may not be 100% accurate because the recipes have not been professionally evaluated nor have they been evaluated by the U.S. FDA.

Vitamins	
Choline 54	**9.82%**
Folate 234µg	**58.50%**
Niacin 2.399mg	**14.99%**
Riboflavin 0.378mg	**29.08%**
Thiamin 0.377mg	**31.42%**
Vitamin B-12 0µg	
Vitamin B-6 0.845mg	**65.00%**
Vitamin D 0IU	
Vitamin E 1	**6.67%**
Vitamin K 1039.6µg	**866.33%**

Minerals

Copper 1.581mg	**175.67%**
Magnesium 106mg	**25.24%**
Phosphorus 243mg	**34.71%**
Selenium 4.5µg	**8.18%**
Zinc 1.55mg	**14.09%**

Other

Caffeine 0
Theobromine 0
Water 469.7g

All nutrient values are calculated from the USDA nutrition database.

Fresh Salsa

A spicy taste of Latin America.

Yields 1 glass.

Ingredients

- Dash of cayenne pepper powder
- 1 stalk celery
- 1 handful cilantro
- 1 clove garlic
- 1 medium onion
- 1 medium sweet bell pepper
- 1 dash salt
- 1 cup cherry tomatoes

Directions

1. Wash the vegetables thoroughly.
2. Put all the ingredients into a juicer and process them.
3. Shake or stir.
4. Serve immediately.

Nutrition Facts (Juiced)

Calories 39
Calories from Fat 5.46

	% Daily Value *
Total Fat 0.61g	1.74%
Saturated Fat 0.11g	0.55%

Monounsaturated Fat 0.126g	
Polyunsaturated Fat 0.209g	
Cholesterol 0mg	
Sodium 165mg	**11.00%**
Potassium 6746mg	**14.34%**
Total Carbohydrate 11.68g	**8.89%**
Dietary Fiber 0.6g	**1.58%**
Sugars 6,05g	
Protein 2.79g	
Vitamin A 157µg	**17.44%**
Vitamin C 64mg	**102.00%**
Calcium 61mg	**6.40%**
Iron 1.28mg	**16.00%**

* The Percent Daily Values are based on a 2,000 calorie diet, so your values may change depending on your calorie needs. The values here may not be 100% accurate because the recipes have not been professionally evaluated nor have they been evaluated by the U.S. FDA.

Vitamins	
Choline 18.5mg	**3.36%**
Folate 62µg	**15.50%**
Niacin 1.511mg	**9.44%**
Riboflavin 0.119mg	**9.15%**
Thiamin 0.122mg	**10.17%**
Vitamin B-12 0µg	
Vitamin B-6 0.375mg	**28.85%**
Vitamin D 0IU	

Vitamin E 1.69mg	**11.27%**
Vitamin K 123.2µg	**102.67%**
Minerals	
Copper 0.201mg	**22.33%**
Magnesium 34mg	**8.10%**
Phosphorus 71mg	**10.14%**
Selenium 0.8µg	**1.45%**
Zinc 0.53mg	**4.82%**
Other	
Caffeine 0mg	
Theobromine 0mg	
Water 252.17g	

All nutrient values are calculated from the USDA nutrition database.

V-7 Cocktail

A smorgasbord of nutrients and goodness.

Yields 1 glass.

Ingredients

- 2 large carrots
- 3 stalks celery
- ½ cucumber
- 2 handfuls parsley
- ½ sweet green pepper
- 1 cup spinach
- 3 tomatoes

Directions

1. Wash the vegetables thoroughly.

2. Put all the ingredients into a juicer and process them.

3. Serve immediately.

Nutrition Facts (Juiced)

Calories 117
Calories from Fat 15.28

	% Daily Value *
Total Fat 1.7g	**4.86%**
Saturated Fat 0.316g	**1.58%**
Monounsaturated Fat 0.313g	
Polyunsaturated Fat 0.602g	

Cholesterol 0mg	
Sodium 241mg	**16.07%**
Potassium 1939mg	**41.26%**
Total Carbohydrate 33.76g	**25.97%**
Dietary Fiber 1.7g	**4.47%**
Sugars 17.35g	
Protein 7.44g	
Vitamin A 1327µg	**147.44%**
Vitamin C 162.3mg	**180.33%**
Calcium 232mg	**23.20%**
Iron 5.75mg	**71.88%**

* The Percent Daily Values are based on a 2,000 calorie diet, so your values may change depending on your calorie needs. The values here may not be 100% accurate because the recipes have not been professionally evaluated nor have they been evaluated by the U.S. FDA.

Vitamins	
Choline 54.2mg	**9.85%**
Folate 244µg	**61.00%**
Niacin 4.146mg	**25.91%**
Riboflavin 0.325mg	**25.00%**
Thiamin 0.307mg	**25.58%**
Vitamin B-12 0µg	
Vitamin B-6 0.672mg	**51.69%**
Vitamin D 0IU	
Vitamin E 3.45mg	**23.00%**
Vitamin K 1113.3µg	**927.75%**

Minerals

Copper 0.426mg	**47.33%**
Magnesium 118mg	**28.10%**
Phosphorus 206mg	**29.43%**
Selenium 1.2µg	**2.18%**
Zinc 1.83mg	**16.64%**

Other

Caffeine 0mg
Theobromine 0mg
Water 669.14g

All nutrient values are calculated from the USDA nutrition database.

Tomato Carrot Celery

The celery mellows out the explosive flavors of the tomato and carrot. Great combo.

Yields 1 glass.

Ingredients

- 3 carrots, topped
- 2 tomatoes
- 3 celery ribs

Directions

1. Wash the vegetables thoroughly.
2. Put all the ingredients into a juicer and process them.
3. Serve immediately.

Spinach Carrot

This is quite alkalizing, aiding digestion

Yields 1 glass.

Ingredients

- 1 handful spinach
- 6 carrots, topped

Directions

1. Wash the vegetables thoroughly.
2. Put all the ingredients into a juicer and process them.
3. Serve immediately.

Beet Carrot

As flavorful as it is colorful.

Yields 1 glass.

Ingredients

- ½ beet
- 6 carrots, topped

Directions

1. Wash the vegetables thoroughly.
2. Put all the ingredients into a juicer and process them.
3. Serve immediately.

Cucumber Tomato

It's amazing how well tomato combines with just about any vegetable under the sun.

Yields 1 glass.

Ingredients

- 1 cucumber
- 1 tomato
- 1 clove garlic, peeled

Directions

1. Wash the vegetables thoroughly.
2. Put all the ingredients into a juicer and process them.
3. Serve immediately.

Spirulina Beet Spinach

Just had to include a recipe with spirulina, a food you nutritionally just can't "beet". This is said to be good for hangovers.

Yields 1 glass.

Ingredients

- 1 beet
- 2 large stalks celery
- 3 cups spinach
- 1 teaspoon dried spirulina

Directions

1. Wash the vegetables thoroughly.
2. Put all the ingredients into a juicer and process them.
3. Serve immediately.

Nutrition Facts (Juiced)

	% Daily Value *
Calories 63	
Calories from Fat 6.58	
Total Fat 0.73g	2.09%
Saturated Fat 0.153g	0.77%
Monounsaturated Fat 0.085g	
Polyunsaturated Fat 0.282g	
Cholesterol 0mg	

Sodium 234mg	**15.60%**
Potassium 1005mg	**21.38%**
Total Carbohydrate 17.05g	**13.12%**
Dietary Fiber 0.9g	**2.37%**
Sugars 10.24g	
Protein 5.32g	
Vitamin A 318µg	**35.33%**
Vitamin C 26.6mg	**29.56%**
Calcium 120mg	**12.00%**
Iron 3.33mg	**41.62%**

* The Percent Daily Values are based on a 2,000 calorie diet, so your values may change depending on your calorie needs. The values here may not be 100% accurate because the recipes have not been professionally evaluated nor have they been evaluated by the U.S. FDA.

Vitamins

Choline 26mg	**4.73%**
Folate 290µg	**72.50%**
Niacin 1.359mg	**8.49%**
Riboflavin 0.278mg	**21.38%**
Thiamin 0.144mg	**12.00%**
Vitamin B-12 0µg	
Vitamin B-6 0.277mg	**21.31%**
Vitamin D 0IU	
Vitamin E 1.65mg	**11.00%**
Vitamin K 331.1µg	**275.92%**

Minerals

Copper 0.304mg	**33.78%**
Magnesium 91mg	**21.67%**
Phosphorus 103mg	**14.71%**
Selenium 2μg	**3.64%**
Zinc 0.91mg	**8.27%**

Other

Caffeine 0mg
Theobromine 0mg
Water 250.45g

All nutrient values are calculated from the USDA nutrition database.

Mixed Recipes

These recipes contain a mix of fruits, vegies, spices or herbs. They tend to have a broad spectrum of nutrients and other beneficial substances, so they're generally well-balanced nutritionally. But they also tend to be a little harder to digest, so it's best to drink them on an empty stomach and allow at least an hour before you eat a meal.

Spinach Splendor

Few types of leafy greens offer more alkalizing green juice with minimal bitterness than spinach. The strong taste of the spinach in this recipe is mellowed by the cucumber.

Yields 1 glass.

Ingredients

- 5 handfuls of spinach
- 1 medium cucumber
- ½ lime (optional)

Directions

1. Wash the vegetables thoroughly.
2. Put all the ingredients into a juicer and process them.
3. OR Squeeze the lime by hand into the finished juice.
4. Serve immediately.

Nutrition Facts (Juiced)

Calories 46

Calories from Fat 5.58

	% Daily Value *
Total Fat 0.62g	1.77%
Saturated Fat 0.138g	0.69%
Monounsaturated Fat 0.024g	
Polyunsaturated Fat 0.225g	
Cholesterol 0mg	
Sodium 74mg	4.93%
Potassium 822mg	17.49%
Total Carbohydrate 13.3g	10.23%
Dietary Fiber 0.5g	1.32%
Sugars 4.28g	
Protein 4.04g	
Vitamin A 421µg	46.78%
Vitamin C 37.3mg	41.44%
Calcium 128mg	12.8%
Iron 3.1mg	38.75%

* The Percent Daily Values are based on a 2,000 calorie diet, so your values may change depending on your calorie needs. The values here may not be 100% accurate because the recipes have not been professionally evaluated nor have they been evaluated by the U.S. FDA.

Vitamins

Choline 30.7mg	**5.58%**
Folate 186μg	**46.5%**
Niacin 0.887mg	**5.54%**
Riboflavin 0.24mg	**18.46%**
Thiamin 0.132mg	**11%**
Vitamin B-12 0μg	
Vitamin B-6 0.265mg	**20.38%**
Vitamin D 0IU	
Vitamin E 1.89mg	**12.6%**
Vitamin K 457.2μg	**381%**

Minerals

Copper 0.215mg	**23.89%**
Magnesium 98mg	**23.33%**
Phosphorus 98mg	**14%**
Selenium 1.6μg	**2.91%**
Zinc 0.91mg	**8.27%**

Other

Caffeine 0mg	
Theobromine 0mg	
Water 301.32g	

All nutrient values are calculated from the USDA nutrition database.

Ginger Beet

Beets and ginger both aid digestion, so give this recipe a try when your stomach is out of sorts.

Yields 1 glass.

Ingredients

- 2 green apples
- ½ medium beet
- 1-inch piece of ginger

Directions

1. Wash the fruits and vegetables thoroughly.
2. Put the ginger into the juicer first so that it lends more of its flavor to the beet and apples. Add the beet and apples and process.
3. Serve immediately.

Nutrition Facts (Juiced)

Calories 163
Calories from Fat 6.91

	% Daily Value *
Total Fat 0.77g	2.2%
Saturated Fat 0.139g	0.7%
Monounsaturated Fat 0.083g	
Polyunsaturated Fat 0.229g	
Cholesterol 0mg	

Sodium 100mg	**6.67%**
Potassium 740mg	**15.74%**
Total Carbohydrate 49.88g	**38.37%**
Dietary Fiber 1.4g	**3.68%**
Sugars 35.04g	
Protein 2.94g	
Vitamin A 10μg	**1.11%**
Vitamin C 18.6mg	**20.67%**
Calcium 38mg	**3.8%**
Iron 1.39mg	**17.38%**

* The Percent Daily Values are based on a 2,000 calorie diet, so your values may change depending on your calorie needs. The values here may not be 100% accurate because the recipes have not been professionally evaluated nor have they been evaluated by the U.S. FDA.

Vitamins	
Choline 20.9mg	**3.8%**
Folate 143μg	**35.75%**
Niacin 0.767mg	**4.79%**
Riboflavin 0.121mg	**9.31%**
Thiamin 0.085mg	**7.08%**
Vitamin B-12 0μg	
Vitamin B-6 0.213mg	**16.38%**
Vitamin D 0IU	
Vitamin E 0.55mg	**3.67%**
Vitamin K 5.9μg	**4.92%**

Minerals

Copper 0.199mg	**22.11%**
Magnesium 48mg	**11.43%**
Phosphorus 83mg	**11.86%**
Selenium 1µg	**1.82%**
Zinc 0.59mg	**5.36%**

Other

Caffeine 0mg	
Theobromine 0mg	
Water 338.55g	

All nutrient values are calculated from the USDA nutrition database.

Carrot Lemon Zest

The tartness of the lemon complements the sweetness of the carrot.

Yields 1 glass.

Ingredients

- 5 medium carrots
- ½ lemon

Directions

1. Wash the carrots thoroughly.
2. Peel the lemon.
3. Put all the ingredients into a juicer and process them.
4. Shake or stir.
5. Serve immediately.

Nutrition Facts (Juiced)

Calories 72
Calories from Fat 5.41

	% Daily Value *
Total Fat 0.6g	**1.71%**
Saturated Fat 0.09g	**0.45%**
Monounsaturated Fat 0.033g	
Polyunsaturated Fat 0.276g	
Cholesterol 0mg	

Sodium 148mg	**9.87%**
Potassium 724mg	**15.4%**
Total Carbohydrate 23.19g	**17.84%**
Dietary Fiber 1g	**2.63%**
Sugars 10.85g	
Protein 2.31g	
Vitamin A 1783μg	**198.11%**
Vitamin C 28.2mg	**31.33%**
Calcium 78mg	**7.8%**
Iron 0.82mg	**10.25%**

* The Percent Daily Values are based on a 2,000 calorie diet, so your values may change depending on your calorie needs. The values here may not be 100% accurate because the recipes have not been professionally evaluated nor have they been evaluated by the U.S. FDA.

Vitamins

Choline 20.3mg	**3.69%**
Folate 44μg	**11%**
Niacin 2.128mg	**13.3%**
Riboflavin 0.13mg	**10%**
Thiamin 0.153mg	**12.75%**
Vitamin B-12 0μg	
Vitamin B-6 0.318mg	**24.46%**
Vitamin D 0IU	
Vitamin E 1.45mg	**9.67%**
Vitamin K 28.2μg	**23.5%**

Minerals

Copper 0.107mg	**11.89%**
Magnesium 28mg	**6.67%**
Phosphorus 79mg	**11.29%**
Selenium 0.3µg	**0.55%**
Zinc 0.53mg	**4.82%**
Other	
Caffeine 0mg	
Theobromine 0mg	
Water 214.66g	

All nutrient values are calculated from the USDA nutrition database.

Beets & Treats

A cornucopia of tastes in this combo.

Yields 1 glass.

Ingredients

- 1 beet
- 2 leaves of red cabbage
- 3 medium carrots
- ½ lemon
- 1 orange
- ¼ pineapple
- 2 handfuls spinach

Directions

1. Wash the fruits and vegetables thoroughly.
2. Put all the ingredients into a juicer and process them.
3. Shake or stir.
4. Serve immediately.

Nutrition Facts (Juiced)

Calories 201
Calories from Fat 9.55

	% Daily Value *
Total Fat 1.06g	3.03%
Saturated Fat 0.149g	0.75%
Monounsaturated Fat 0.109g	

Polyunsaturated Fat 0.397g	
Cholesterol 0mg	
Sodium 218mg	**14.53%**
Potassium 1418mg	**30.17%**
Total Carbohydrate 60.77g	**46.75%**
Dietary Fiber 1.9g	**5%**
Sugars 40.08g	
Protein 6.47g	
Vitamin A 1252µg	**139.11%**
Vitamin C 171.2mg	**190.22%**
Calcium 170mg	**17%**
Iron 3.14mg	**39.25%**

* The Percent Daily Values are based on a 2,000 calorie diet, so your values may change depending on your calorie needs. The values here may not be 100% accurate because the recipes have not been professionally evaluated nor have they been evaluated by the U.S. FDA.

Vitamins	
Choline 45.5mg	**8.27%**
Folate 294µg	**73.5%**
Niacin 3.051mg	**19.07%**
Riboflavin 0.291mg	**22.38%**
Thiamin 0.379mg	**31.58%**
Vitamin B-12 0µg	
Vitamin B-6 0.609mg	**46.85%**
Vitamin D 0IU	
Vitamin E 1.88mg	**12.53%**

Vitamin K 203.2μg	**169.33%**
Minerals	
Copper 0.425mg	**47.22%**
Magnesium 104mg	**24.76%**
Phosphorus 147mg	**21%**
Selenium 2.1μg	**3.82%**
Zinc 1.23mg	**11.18%**
Other	
Caffeine 0mg	
Theobromine 0mg	
Water 513.65g	

All nutrient values are calculated from the USDA nutrition database.

Apple Melon Kale

An unusual combination and a distinctive flavor.

Yields 1 glass.

Ingredients

- 2 apples, cored
- ½ cantaloupe
- ½ honeydew
- 6 kale leaves
- 6 Swiss chard leaves

Directions

1. Wash the apples, kale and chard thoroughly.
2. Put all the ingredients into a juicer and process them.
3. Shake or stir.
4. Serve immediately.

Nutrition Facts (Juiced)

Calories 417	
Calories from Fat 28.78	
	% Daily Value *
Total Fat 3.2g	**9.14%**
Saturated Fat 0.534g	**2.67%**
Monounsaturated Fat 0.194g	
Polyunsaturated Fat 1.189g	
Cholesterol 0mg	

Sodium 599mg	**39.93%**
Potassium 3296mg	**70.13%**
Total Carbohydrate 112.08g	**86.22%**
Dietary Fiber 2.1g	5.53%
Sugars 80.25g	
Protein 14.62g	
Vitamin A 1699µg	**188.78%**
Vitamin C 400.1mg	**444.56%**
Calcium 383mg	**38.3%**
Iron 7.26mg	**90.75%**

* The Percent Daily Values are based on a 2,000 calorie diet, so your values may change depending on your calorie needs. The values here may not be 100% accurate because the recipes have not been professionally evaluated nor have they been evaluated by the U.S. FDA.

Vitamins	
Choline 93.7mg	**17.04%**
Folate 207µg	**51.75%**
Niacin 5.799mg	**36.24%**
Riboflavin 0.529mg	**40.69%**
Thiamin 0.535mg	**44.58%**
Vitamin B-12 0µg	
Vitamin B-6 1.236mg	**95.08%**
Vitamin D 0IU	
Vitamin E 4.46mg	**29.73%**
Vitamin K 2732.8µg	**2277.33%**
Minerals	

Copper 2.82mg	**313.33%**
Magnesium 313mg	**74.52%**
Phosphorus 334mg	**47.71%**
Selenium 7µg	**12.73%**
Zinc 2.4mg	**21.82%**

Other

Caffeine 0mg	
Theobromine 0mg	
Water 1104.91g	

All nutrient values are calculated from the USDA nutrition database.

Green Citrus

Deliciously tart. Perfect for a hot summer evening.

Yields 1 glass.

Ingredients

- 1 bunch chard (can substitute with collards, spinach or kale)
- 2 cucumbers
- ½ bunch parsley (can substitute with cilantro or mint)
- 1 lemon, peeled
- 1 lime, peeled
- 1 green apple, cored

Directions

1. Wash the chard, cucumbers and parsley thoroughly.
2. Put all the ingredients into a juicer and process them, preferably in this order: greens, herbs, lemon, lime, cucumber.
3. Shake or stir.
4. Serve immediately.

Nutrition Facts (Juiced)

Calories 167
Calories from Fat 15.42

	% Daily Value *
Total Fat 1.71g	**4.89%**
Saturated Fat 0.348g	**1.74%**
Monounsaturated Fat 0.279g	
Polyunsaturated Fat 0.468g	

Cholesterol 0mg	
Sodium 470mg	31.33%
Potassium 1915mg	40.74%
Total Carbohydrate 52.48g	40.37%
Dietary Fiber 1.8g	4.74%
Sugars 24.75g	
Protein 9.03g	
Vitamin A 864µg	96%
Vitamin C 183.1mg	203.44%
Calcium 276mg	27.6%
Iron 8.74mg	109.25%

* The Percent Daily Values are based on a 2,000 calorie diet, so your values may change depending on your calorie needs. The values here may not be 100% accurate because the recipes have not been professionally evaluated nor have they been evaluated by the U.S. FDA.

Vitamins	
Choline 77.1mg	14.02%
Folate 150µg	37.5%
Niacin 2.159mg	13.49%
Riboflavin 0.423mg	32.54%
Thiamin 0.292mg	24.33%
Vitamin B-12 0µg	
Vitamin B-6 0.52mg	40%
Vitamin D 0IU	
Vitamin E 4.72mg	31.47%
Vitamin K 2606.5µg	2172.08%

Minerals

Copper 0.692mg	**76.89%**
Magnesium 257mg	**61.19%**
Phosphorus 253mg	**36.14%**
Selenium 3.5μg	**6.36%**
Zinc 2.26mg	**20.55%**

Other

Caffeine 0mg
Theobromine 0mg
Water 820.67g

All nutrient values are calculated from the USDA nutrition database.

Pepper Carrot Apple

Bell peppers not only provide a ton of vitamins and minerals, but also have anti-fungal and anti-bacterial properties.

Yields 1 glass.

Ingredients

- 2 large carrots, ends trimmed
- 2 large celery stalks
- 1/2 beet
- 1/4 green bell pepper
- 1/4 apple
- ½ teaspoon fresh ginger, chopped

Directions

1. Wash the fruits and vegetables thoroughly.
2. Put all the ingredients into a juicer and process them.
3. Shake or stir.
4. Serve immediately.

Nutrition Facts (Juiced)

Calories 82
Calories from Fat 5.9

	% Daily Value *
Total Fat 0.66g	**1.89%**
Saturated Fat 0.116g	**0.58%**
Monounsaturated Fat 0.074g	

Polyunsaturated Fat 0.292g

Cholesterol 0mg	
Sodium 190mg	**12.67%**
Potassium 841mg	**17.89%**
Total Carbohydrate 24.44g	**18.8%**
Dietary Fiber 1g	2.63%
Sugars 14.59g	
Protein 2.84g	
Vitamin A 871µg	96.78%
Vitamin C 30.9mg	34.33%
Calcium 84mg	8.4%
Iron 1.12mg	14%

* The Percent Daily Values are based on a 2,000 calorie diet, so your values may change depending on your calorie needs. The values here may not be 100% accurate because the recipes have not been professionally evaluated nor have they been evaluated by the U.S. FDA.

Vitamins	
Choline 21.5mg	**3.91%**
Folate 130µg	**32.5%**
Niacin 1.743mg	**10.89%**
Riboflavin 0.154mg	**11.85%**
Thiamin 0.126mg	**10.5%**
Vitamin B-12 0µg	
Vitamin B-6 0.363mg	**27.92%**
Vitamin D 0IU	
Vitamin E 1.09mg	**7.27%**

Vitamin K 42.3μg	**35.25%**

Minerals

Copper 0.161mg	**17.89%**
Magnesium 42mg	**10%**
Phosphorus 91mg	**13%**
Selenium 1μg	**1.82%**
Zinc 0.65mg	**5.91%**

Other

Caffeine 0mg
Theobromine 0mg
Water 275.34g

All nutrient values are calculated from the USDA nutrition database.

Tomato Strawberry Ginger

After juicing this, you can save the pulp from the carrots and tomatoes and use it for soup, adding broth, onion and garlic to it.

Yields 1 glass.

Ingredients

- 3 large carrots, topped
- 1 large tomato
- 8 large strawberries
- 1 lime, sliced
- 1 one-inch piece fresh ginger
- 1 apple
- 1 large red bell pepper, stemmed and seeded

Directions

1. Wash the fruits and vegetables thoroughly.
2. Put all the ingredients into a juicer and process them.
3. Shake or stir.
4. Serve immediately.

Nutrition Facts (Juiced)

Calories 171
Calories from Fat 12.91

	% Daily Value *
Total Fat 1.43g	**4.09%**
Saturated Fat 0.196g	**0.98%**

Monounsaturated Fat 0.152g	
Polyunsaturated Fat 0.601g	
Cholesterol 0mg	
Sodium 116mg	**7.73%**
Potassium 1232mg	**26.21%**
Total Carbohydrate 53.97g	**41.52%**
Dietary Fiber 1.8g	**4.74%**
Sugars 30.43g	
Protein 4.32g	
Vitamin A 1330μg	**147.78%**
Vitamin C 123.6mg	**137.33%**
Calcium 107mg	**10.7%**
Iron 1.83mg	**22.88%**

* The Percent Daily Values are based on a 2,000 calorie diet, so your values may change depending on your calorie needs. The values here may not be 100% accurate because the recipes have not been professionally evaluated nor have they been evaluated by the U.S. FDA.

Vitamins

Choline 40.6mg	**7.38%**
Folate 91μg	**22.75%**
Niacin 3.174mg	**19.84%**
Riboflavin 0.193mg	**14.85%**
Thiamin 0.226mg	**18.83%**
Vitamin B-12 0μg	
Vitamin B-6 0.555mg	**42.69%**
Vitamin D 0IU	

Vitamin E 2.45mg	**16.33%**
Vitamin K 37.2μg	**31%**
Minerals	
Copper 0.316mg	**35.11%**
Magnesium 65mg	**15.48%**
Phosphorus 141mg	**20.14%**
Selenium 0.9μg	**1.64%**
Zinc 0.94mg	**8.55%**
Other	
Caffeine 0mg	
Theobromine 0mg	
Water 526.54g	

All nutrient values are calculated from the USDA nutrition database.

Cucumber Kiwi Mint

An interesting taste to an unusual combination.

Yields 1 glass.

Ingredients

- ½ lemon, peeled
- ½ cucumber
- 1 cup green grapes
- 1 wedge honeydew melon
- 1 kiwi
- 1 celery stalk
- 1 handful fresh mint

Directions

1. Wash the fruits and vegetables thoroughly.
2. Put all the ingredients into a juicer and process them.
3. Shake or stir.
4. Serve immediately.

Nutrition Facts (Juiced)

Calories 111
Calories from Fat 8.62

	% Daily Value *
Total Fat 0.96g	**2.74%**
Saturated Fat 0.119g	**0.6%**
Monounsaturated Fat 0.044g	

Polyunsaturated Fat 0.288g

Cholesterol 0mg	
Sodium 47mg	**3.13%**
Potassium 803mg	**17.09%**
Total Carbohydrate 33.46g	**25.74%**
Dietary Fiber 0.9g	2.37%
Sugars 16	
Protein 2.87g	
Vitamin A 19μg	2.11%
Vitamin C 84.4mg	93.78%
Calcium 83mg	8.3%
Iron 1.04mg	13%

* The Percent Daily Values are based on a 2,000 calorie diet, so your values may change depending on your calorie needs. The values here may not be 100% accurate because the recipes have not been professionally evaluated nor have they been evaluated by the U.S. FDA.

Vitamins

Choline 22	4%
Folate 56μg	14%
Niacin 0.858mg	5.36%
Riboflavin 0.083mg	6.38%
Thiamin 0.102mg	8.5%
Vitamin B-12 0μg	
Vitamin B-6 0.216mg	16.62%
Vitamin D 0IU	
Vitamin E 1	6.67%

Vitamin K 48	**40%**
Minerals	
Copper 0.229mg	**25.44%**
Magnesium 47mg	**11.19%**
Phosphorus 81mg	**11.57%**
Selenium 1	**1.82%**
Zinc 0.5mg	**4.55%**
Other	
Caffeine 0	
Theobromine 0	
Water 347.17g	

All nutrient values are calculated from the USDA nutrition database.

Spinach Ginger Lemon

High in enzymes and vitamins.

Yields 1 glass.

Ingredients

- 1 handful spinach
- ½ lime, peeled
- 1 lemon, peeled
- 1 large cucumber
- 1 apple
- 1 small piece ginger

Directions

1. Wash the fruits and vegetables thoroughly.
2. Put all the ingredients into a juicer and process them.
3. Shake or stir.
4. Serve immediately.

Nutrition Facts (Juiced)

Calories 102
Calories from Fat 6.51

	% Daily Value *
Total Fat 0.72g	**2.06%**
Saturated Fat 0.156g	0.78%
Monounsaturated Fat 0.038g	
Polyunsaturated Fat 0.218g	

Cholesterol 0mg	
Sodium 21mg	1.4%
Potassium 645mg	13.72%
Total Carbohydrate 33.03g	25.41%
Dietary Fiber 0.9g	2.37%
Sugars 18.33g	
Protein 2.9g	
Vitamin A 97µg	10.78%
Vitamin C 45.3mg	50.33%
Calcium 78mg	7.8%
Iron 1.63mg	20.38%

* The Percent Daily Values are based on a 2,000 calorie diet, so your values may change depending on your calorie needs. The values here may not be 100% accurate because the recipes have not been professionally evaluated nor have they been evaluated by the U.S. FDA.

Vitamins	
Choline 25.1mg	**4.56%**
Folate 59µg	**14.75%**
Niacin 0.574mg	**3.59%**
Riboflavin 0.15mg	**11.54%**
Thiamin 0.117mg	**9.75%**
Vitamin B-12 0µg	
Vitamin B-6 0.221mg	**17%**
Vitamin D 0IU	
Vitamin E 0.77mg	**5.13%**
Vitamin K 122µg	**101.67%**

Minerals

Copper 0.185mg	**20.56%**
Magnesium 54mg	**12.86%**
Phosphorus 86mg	**12.29%**
Selenium 1.1µg	**2%**
Zinc 0.63mg	**5.73%**

Other

Caffeine 0mg	
Theobromine 0mg	
Water 386.45g	

All nutrient values are calculated from the USDA nutrition database.

Celery Citrus Cucumber Cocktail

In terms of nutrition, this one brings down the house.

Yields 1 glass.

Ingredients

- 2 medium apples, cored
- 2 stalks celery
- 1 cucumber
- 5 leaves kale
- ½ lemon
- 2 oranges, peeled

Directions

1. Wash the fruits and vegetables thoroughly.
2. Put all the ingredients into a juicer and process them.
3. Shake or stir.
4. Serve immediately.

Nutrition Facts (Juiced)

Calories 102
Calories from Fat 6.51

	% Daily Value *
Total Fat 0.72g	**2.06%**
Saturated Fat 0.156g	**0.78%**
Monounsaturated Fat 0.038g	
Polyunsaturated Fat 0.218g	

Cholesterol 0mg	
Sodium 21mg	1.4%
Potassium 645mg	13.72%
Total Carbohydrate 33.03g	25.41%
Dietary Fiber 0.9g	2.37%
Sugars 18.33g	
Protein 2.9g	
Vitamin A 97μg	10.78%
Vitamin C 45.3mg	50.33%
Calcium 78mg	7.8%
Iron 1.63mg	20.38%

* The Percent Daily Values are based on a 2,000 calorie diet, so your values may change depending on your calorie needs. The values here may not be 100% accurate because the recipes have not been professionally evaluated nor have they been evaluated by the U.S. FDA.

Vitamins	
Choline 25.1mg	4.56%
Folate 59μg	14.75%
Niacin 0.574mg	3.59%
Riboflavin 0.15mg	11.54%
Thiamin 0.117mg	9.75%
Vitamin B-12 0μg	
Vitamin B-6 0.221mg	17%
Vitamin D 0IU	
Vitamin E 0.77mg	5.13%
Vitamin K 122μg	101.67%

Minerals

Copper 0.185mg	**20.56%**
Magnesium 54mg	**12.86%**
Phosphorus 86mg	**12.29%**
Selenium 1.1µg	**2%**
Zinc 0.63mg	**5.73%**

Other

Caffeine 0mg
Theobromine 0mg
Water 386.45g

All nutrient values are calculated from the USDA nutrition database.

Strawberry Pineapple Mint

Three distinct and excellent flavors, but the whole is even better than the sum of its parts.

Yields 1 glass.

Ingredients

- ½ large pineapple, peeled, cored and cut into cubes
- 1 cup strawberries
- 1 pear
- 30 mint leaves

Directions

1. Wash the pear and strawberries thoroughly.
2. Put all the ingredients into a juicer and process them.
3. Shake or stir.
4. Serve immediately.

Nutrition Facts (Juiced)

Calories 225
Calories from Fat 7.8

	% Daily Value *
Total Fat 0.87g	**2.49%**
Saturated Fat 0.074g	**0.37%**
Monounsaturated Fat 0.19g	
Polyunsaturated Fat 0.405g	
Cholesterol 0mg	

Sodium 6mg	**0.4%**
Potassium 650mg	**13.83%**
Total Carbohydrate 68.43g	**52.64%**
Dietary Fiber 1.5g	**3.95%**
Sugars 48	
Protein 2.87g	
Vitamin A 14μg	**1.56%**
Vitamin C 216.4mg	**240.44%**
Calcium 71mg	**7.1%**
Iron 1.61mg	**20.13%**

* The Percent Daily Values are based on a 2,000 calorie diet, so your values may change depending on your calorie needs. The values here may not be 100% accurate because the recipes have not been professionally evaluated nor have they been evaluated by the U.S. FDA.

Vitamins

Choline 30	**5.45%**
Folate 91μg	**22.75%**
Niacin 2.191mg	**13.69%**
Riboflavin 0.159mg	**12.23%**
Thiamin 0.29mg	**24.17%**
Vitamin B-12 0μg	
Vitamin B-6 0.44mg	**33.85%**
Vitamin D 0IU	
Vitamin E 1	**6.67%**
Vitamin K 10	**8.33%**

Minerals

Copper 0.502mg	**55.78%**
Magnesium 61mg	**14.52%**
Phosphorus 65mg	**9.29%**
Selenium 1	**1.82%**
Zinc 0.66mg	**6%**

Other

Caffeine 0	
Theobromine 0	
Water 469.52g	

All nutrient values are calculated from the USDA nutrition database.

Tropical Green

Mangoes are among the best providers of beta-carotene.

Yields 1 glass.

Ingredients

- ½ thumb ginger root
- 4 leaves kale
- 1 mango, without refuse
- 1 orange, peeled
- 1 cup pineapple chunks

Directions

1. Wash the kale thoroughly.
2. Put all the ingredients into a juicer and process them.
3. Shake or stir.
4. Serve immediately.

Nutrition Facts (Juiced)

Calories 259
Calories from Fat 18.79

	% Daily Value *
Total Fat 2.09g	**5.97%**
Saturated Fat 0.343g	**1.72%**
Monounsaturated Fat 0.424g	
Polyunsaturated Fat 0.574g	
Cholesterol 0mg	

Sodium 42mg	**2.80%**
Potassium 1159mg	**24.66%**
Total Carbohydrate 68.35g	**52.58%**
Dietary Fiber 1g	**2.63%**
Sugars 49.93	
Protein 7.53g	
Vitamin A 628µg	69.78%
Vitamin C 294.6mg	327.33%
Calcium 216mg	21.60%
Iron 2.27mg	28.38%

* The Percent Daily Values are based on a 2,000 calorie diet, so your values may change depending on your calorie needs. The values here may not be 100% accurate because the recipes have not been professionally evaluated nor have they been evaluated by the U.S. FDA.

Vitamins	
Choline 32.3	5.87%
Folate 173µg	43.25%
Niacin 3.383mg	21.14%
Riboflavin 0.283mg	21.77%
Thiamin 0.325mg	27.08%
Vitamin B-12 0µg	
Vitamin B-6 0.729mg	56.08%
Vitamin D 0IU	
Vitamin E 2.28	15.20%
Vitamin K 701.4	584.50%
Minerals	

Copper 1.906mg	**211.78%**
Magnesium 94mg	**22.38%**
Phosphorus 145mg	**20.71%**
Selenium 2.8	**5.09%**
Zinc 0.97mg	**8.82%**

Other

Caffeine 0mg
Theobromine 0mg
Water 442.91g
All nutrient values are calculated from the USDA nutrition database.

Apple Celery Ginger

The lemon-ginger combination packs a flavor punch.

Yields 2 glasses (32 oz.).

Ingredients

- 3 medium apples, cored
- 3 stalks celery
- 1/2 cucumber
- ½ thumb ginger root
- 4 leaves kale
- 1 lemon, quartered
- 1 large orange, peeled

Directions

1. Wash the fruits and vegetables thoroughly.
2. Put all the ingredients into a juicer and process them.
3. Shake or stir.
4. Serve immediately.

Nutrition Facts (Juiced)

Calories 305
Calories from Fat 20.2

	% Daily Value *
Total Fat 2.24g	**6.40%**
Saturated Fat 0.344g	1.72%
Monounsaturated Fat 0.173g	

Polyunsaturated Fat 0.747g	
Cholesterol 0mg	
Sodium 153mg	**10.20%**
Potassium 1718mg	**36.55%**
Total Carbohydrate 89.58g	**68.91%**
Dietary Fiber 2.3g	**6.05%**
Sugars 51.13	
Protein 8.61g	
Vitamin A 551µg	**61.22%**
Vitamin C 232.8mg	**258.6%**
Calcium 304mg	**30.40%**
Iron 2.89mg	**36.12%**

* The Percent Daily Values are based on a 2,000 calorie diet, so your values may change depending on your calorie needs. The values here may not be 100% accurate because the recipes have not been professionally evaluated nor have they been evaluated by the U.S. FDA.

Vitamins	
Choline 42.8	**7.78%**
Folate 142µg	**35.50%**
Niacin 2.328mg	**14.55%**
Riboflavin 0.40mg	**30.85%**
Thiamin 0.36mg	**30.00%**
Vitamin B-12 0µg	
Vitamin B-6 0.687mg	**52.85%**
Vitamin D 0IU	
Vitamin E 1.4	**9.33%**

Vitamin K 755.8	**629.83%**
Minerals	
Copper 1.754mg	**194.89%**
Magnesium 113mg	**26.90%**
Phosphorus 217mg	**31.00%**
Selenium 2.6.8	**4.73%**
Zinc 1.23mg	**11.18%**
Other	
Caffeine 0mg	
Theobromine 0mg	
Water 792.44g	

All nutrient values are calculated from the USDA nutrition database.

Pineapple Broccoli Cucumber

Refreshing.

Yields 1 glass.

Ingredients

- 7 ounces pineapple
- 3 ½ ounces broccoli
- 3 ½ ounces cucumber
- 1 kiwi, peeled

Directions

1. Wash the fruits and vegetables thoroughly.
2. Put all the ingredients into a juicer and process them.
3. Shake or stir.
4. Serve immediately.

Nutrition Facts (Juiced)

Calories 102
Calories from Fat 6.43

	% Daily Value *
Total Fat 0.71g	**2.03%**
Saturated Fat 0.075g	0.38%
Monounsaturated Fat 0.049g	
Polyunsaturated Fat 0.231g	
Cholesterol 0mg	
Sodium 27mg	**1.8%**

Potassium 587mg	**12.49%**
Total Carbohydrate 29.18g	**22.45%**
Dietary Fiber 0.7g	**1.84%**
Sugars 18.01g	
Protein 3.53g	
Vitamin A 30µg	**3.33%**
Vitamin C 163.4mg	**181.56%**
Calcium 74mg	**7.4%**
Iron 1.17mg	**14.63%**

* The Percent Daily Values are based on a 2,000 calorie diet, so your values may change depending on your calorie needs. The values here may not be 100% accurate because the recipes have not been professionally evaluated nor have they been evaluated by the U.S. FDA.

Vitamins	
Choline 26.8mg	**4.87%**
Folate 81µg	**20.25%**
Niacin 1.247mg	**7.79%**
Riboflavin 0.151mg	**11.62%**
Thiamin 0.171mg	**14.25%**
Vitamin B-12 0µg	
Vitamin B-6 0.306mg	**23.54%**
Vitamin D 0IU	
Vitamin E 1.28mg	**8.53%**
Vitamin K 100.4µg	**83.67%**

Minerals

Copper 0.25mg	**27.78%**
Magnesium 45mg	**10.71%**
Phosphorus 86mg	**12.29%**
Selenium 2.1µg	**3.82%**
Zinc 0.62mg	**5.64%**

Other

Caffeine 0mg
Theobromine 0mg
Water 261.6g

All nutrient values are calculated from the USDA nutrition database.

Carrot Pineapple Chili

This has lots of vitamin C. The chili offers a nice kick and helps speed up metabolism.

Yields 1 glass.

Ingredients

- 3 large carrots
- 3 slices pineapple
- ½ lime, peeled
- ½ small chili

Directions

1. Wash the carrots and chili thoroughly.

2. Put the carrots, pineapple and lime into a juicer and process them. Then add the chili and a couple ice cubes and put everything into a blender.

3. Serve immediately.

Nutrition Facts (Juiced)

Calories 135
Calories from Fat 6.09

	% Daily Value *
Total Fat 0.68g	1.94%
Saturated Fat 0.082g	0.41%
Monounsaturated Fat 0.052g	
Polyunsaturated Fat 0.29g	
Cholesterol 0mg	

Sodium 108mg	**7.2%**
Potassium 741mg	**15.77%**
Total Carbohydrate 41.21g	**31.7%**
Dietary Fiber 1.1g	**2.89%**
Sugars 25.61g	
Protein 2.76g	
Vitamin A 1274µg	**141.56%**
Vitamin C 118.2mg	**131.33%**
Calcium 82mg	**8.2%**
Iron 1.24mg	**15.5%**

* The Percent Daily Values are based on a 2,000 calorie diet, so your values may change depending on your calorie needs. The values here may not be 100% accurate because the recipes have not been professionally evaluated nor have they been evaluated by the U.S. FDA.

Vitamins

Choline 25.6mg	**4.65%**
Folate 65µg	**16.25%**
Niacin 2.572mg	**16.08%**
Riboflavin 0.16mg	**12.31%**
Thiamin 0.255mg	**21.25%**
Vitamin B-12 0µg	
Vitamin B-6 0.48mg	**36.92%**
Vitamin D 0IU	
Vitamin E 1.17mg	**7.8%**
Vitamin K 23.1µg	**19.25%**

Minerals

Copper 0.294mg	**32.67%**
Magnesium 44mg	**10.48%**
Phosphorus 77mg	**11%**
Selenium 0.5μg	**0.91%**
Zinc 0.63mg	**5.73%**
Other	
Caffeine 0mg	
Theobromine 0mg	
Water 316.99g	

All nutrient values are calculated from the USDA nutrition database.

Ginger Pear Celery

Pears serve as a gentle laxative and celery as a mild diuretic, so this juice is a great cleanser. Ginger aids digestion.

Yields 1 glass.

Ingredients

- 1 small pear
- 2 medium stalks celery
- 1 one-inch piece fresh ginger root

Directions

1. Wash the fruits and vegetables thoroughly.
2. Put all the ingredients into a juicer and process them.
3. Shake or stir.
4. Serve immediately.

Nutrition Facts (Juiced)

Calories 65
Calories from Fat 3.3

	% Daily Value *
Total Fat 0.37g	1.06%
Saturated Fat 0.08g	0.4%
Monounsaturated Fat 0.131g	
Polyunsaturated Fat 0.167g	
Cholesterol 0mg	
Sodium 48mg	3.2%

Potassium 335mg	**7.13%**
Total Carbohydrate 20.43g	**15.72%**
Dietary Fiber 0.6g	**1.58%**
Sugars 11.41g	
Protein 1.07g	
Vitamin A 13μg	**1.44%**
Vitamin C 7mg	**7.78%**
Calcium 34mg	**3.4%**
Iron 0.4mg	**5%**

* The Percent Daily Values are based on a 2,000 calorie diet, so your values may change depending on your calorie needs. The values here may not be 100% accurate because the recipes have not been professionally evaluated nor have they been evaluated by the U.S. FDA.

Vitamins	
Choline 13.5mg	**2.45%**
Folate 29μg	**7.25%**
Niacin 0.472mg	**2.95%**
Riboflavin 0.065mg	**5%**
Thiamin 0.028mg	**2.33%**
Vitamin B-12 0μg	
Vitamin B-6 0.098mg	**7.54%**
Vitamin D 0IU	
Vitamin E 0.32mg	**2.13%**
Vitamin K 21μg	**17.5%**

Minerals

Copper 0.143mg	**15.89%**
Magnesium 21mg	**5%**
Phosphorus 32mg	**4.57%**
Selenium 0.4µg	**0.73%**
Zinc 0.23mg	**2.09%**

Other

Caffeine 0mg
Theobromine 0mg
Water 153.68g

All nutrient values are calculated from the USDA nutrition database.

Spicy Lemonade

Another great cleanser, as both lemons and apples possess cleansing properties.

Yields 1 glass.

Ingredients

- 3 apples, cored
- ½ lemon, peeled
- 1 yellow pepper
- 1-inch cube ginger root

Directions

1. Wash the fruits and vegetables thoroughly.
2. Put all the ingredients into a juicer and process them.
3. Shake or stir.
4. Serve immediately.

Nutrition Facts (Juiced)

Calories 187
Calories from Fat 8.23

	% Daily Value *
Total Fat 0.91g	2.6%
Saturated Fat 0.158g	0.79%
Monounsaturated Fat 0.059g	
Polyunsaturated Fat 0.284g	
Cholesterol 0mg	

Sodium 7mg	**0.47%**
Potassium 545mg	**11.6%**
Total Carbohydrate 58.93g	**45.33%**
Dietary Fiber 1.5g	**3.95%**
Sugars 41.17g	
Protein 1.67g	
Vitamin A 19μg	**2.11%**
Vitamin C 46.7mg	**51.89%**
Calcium 33mg	**3.3%**
Iron 0.77mg	**9.63%**

* The Percent Daily Values are based on a 2,000 calorie diet, so your values may change depending on your calorie needs. The values here may not be 100% accurate because the recipes have not been professionally evaluated nor have they been evaluated by the U.S. FDA.

Vitamins

Choline 20.3mg	**3.69%**
Folate 26μg	**6.5%**
Niacin 0.7mg	**4.38%**
Riboflavin 0.12mg	**9.23%**
Thiamin 0.092mg	**7.67%**
Vitamin B-12 0μg	
Vitamin B-6 0.298mg	**22.92%**
Vitamin D 0IU	
Vitamin E 0.85mg	**5.67%**
Vitamin K 10.3μg	**8.58%**

Minerals

Copper 0.17mg	**18.89%**
Magnesium 31mg	**7.38%**
Phosphorus 56mg	**8%**
Selenium 0.3μg	**0.55%**
Zinc 0.28mg	**2.55%**

Other

Caffeine 0mg
Theobromine 0mg
Water 375.62g

All nutrient values are calculated from the USDA nutrition database.

Carrot Spinach Citrus

This juice can help boost your immune system and help you handle stress better.

Yields 1 glass.

Ingredients

- 2 oranges, peeled
- ½ lemon
- 1/2 beet root
- 4 handfuls spinach
- 3 stalks celery
- 2 small carrots
- 1-inch cube ginger root

Directions

1. Wash the fruits and vegetables thoroughly.
2. Put all the ingredients into a juicer and process them.
3. Shake or stir.
4. Serve immediately.

Nutrition Facts (Juiced)

Calories 189
Calories from Fat 12.87

	% Daily Value *
Total Fat 1.43g	**4.09%**
Saturated Fat 0.242g	**1.21%**

Monounsaturated Fat 0.153g	
Polyunsaturated Fat 0.548g	
Cholesterol 0mg	
Sodium 310mg	**20.67%**
Potassium 1884mg	**40.09%**
Total Carbohydrate 57.14g	**43.95%**
Dietary Fiber 2.2g	**5.79%**
Sugars 33.53g	
Protein 7.76g	
Vitamin A 2023μg	**224.78%**
Vitamin C 151mg	**167.78%**
Calcium 262mg	**26.2%**
Iron 3.61mg	**45.13%**

* The Percent Daily Values are based on a 2,000 calorie diet, so your values may change depending on your calorie needs. The values here may not be 100% accurate because the recipes have not been professionally evaluated nor have they been evaluated by the U.S. FDA.

Vitamins	
Choline 61.5mg	**11.18%**
Folate 331μg	**82.75%**
Niacin 3.6mg	**22.5%**
Riboflavin 0.405mg	**31.15%**
Thiamin 0.397mg	**33.08%**
Vitamin B-12 0μg	
Vitamin B-6 0.674mg	**51.85%**
Vitamin D 0IU	

Vitamin E 3.4mg	**22.67%**
Vitamin K 388.9μg	**324.08%**

Minerals

Copper 0.387mg	**43%**
Magnesium 130mg	**30.95%**
Phosphorus 184mg	**26.29%**
Selenium 2.8μg	**5.09%**
Zinc 1.37mg	**12.45%**

Other

Caffeine 0mg
Theobromine 0mg
Water 571.2g

All nutrient values are calculated from the USDA nutrition database.

Mean Green

Joe Cross's somewhat famous recipe for cleansing. Tastes good, especially for such a good cleanser.

Yields 1 glass.

Ingredients

- 2 medium apples
- 4 stalks celery
- 1 cucumber
- 1 thumb ginger root
- ½ lemon
- 6 leaves kale

Directions

1. Wash the fruits and vegetables thoroughly.
2. Put all the ingredients into a juicer and process them.
3. Shake or stir.
4. Serve immediately.

Nutrition Facts (Juiced)

Calories 246
Calories from Fat 22.96

	% Daily Value *
Total Fat 2.55g	**7.29%**
Saturated Fat 0.404g	**2.02%**
Monounsaturated Fat 0.191g	

Polyunsaturated Fat 0.888g

Cholesterol 0mg	
Sodium 209mg	**13.93%**
Potassium 1880mg	**40.00%**
Total Carbohydrate 66.75g	**51.35%**
Dietary Fiber 1.6g	**4.21%**
Sugars 34.29g	
Protein 10.19g	
Vitamin A 793µg	**88.11%**
Vitamin C 216mg	**240.00%**
Calcium 352mg	**35.20%**
Iron 3.69mg	**46.12%**

* The Percent Daily Values are based on a 2,000 calorie diet, so your values may change depending on your calorie needs. The values here may not be 100% accurate because the recipes have not been professionally evaluated nor have they been evaluated by the U.S. FDA.

Vitamins

Choline 38.6mg	**7.02%**
Folate 138µg	**34.50%**
Niacin 2.637mg	**16.48%**
Riboflavin 0.441mg	**33.92%**
Thiamin 0.315mg	**26.25%**
Vitamin B-12 0µg	
Vitamin B-6 0.77mg	**59.23%**
Vitamin D 0IU	
Vitamin E 1.09mg	**7.27%**

Vitamin K 1128.7µg	**940.58%**
Minerals	
Copper 2.47mg	**274.44%**
Magnesium 139mg	**33.10%**
Phosphorus 267mg	**38.14%**
Selenium 2.9µg	**5.27%**
Zinc 1.65mg	**15.00%**
Other	
Caffeine 0mg	
Theobromine 0mg	
Water 752.62g	

All nutrient values are calculated from the USDA nutrition database.

The Any Time Cocktail

Three days' worth of Vitamin C.

Yields 2 glasses (32 oz.).

Ingredients

- 2 medium apples, cored
- 2 stalks celery
- 1 cucumber
- 5 leaves kale
- ½ lemon
- 2 oranges, peeled
- 1 handful parsley

Directions

1. Wash the fruits and vegetables thoroughly.
2. Put all the ingredients into a juicer and process them.
3. Shake or stir.
4. Serve immediately.

Nutrition Facts (Juiced)

Calories 287
Calories from Fat 21.86

	% Daily Value *
Total Fat 2.43g	**6.94%**
Saturated Fat 0.36g	**1.80%**
Monounsaturated Fat 0.238g	

Polyunsaturated Fat 0.762g

Cholesterol 0mg	
Sodium 114mg	7.60%
Potassium 1857mg	39.51%
Total Carbohydrate 81.28g	62.52%
Dietary Fiber 2g	5.26%
Sugars 49.14g	
Protein 10.54g	
Vitamin A 781µg	86.78%
Vitamin C 316.7mg	351.89%
Calcium 375mg	37.50%
Iron 4.9mg	61.25%

* The Percent Daily Values are based on a 2,000 calorie diet, so your values may change depending on your calorie needs. The values here may not be 100% accurate because the recipes have not been professionally evaluated nor have they been evaluated by the U.S. FDA.

Vitamins	
Choline 45.2mg	8.22%
Folate 181µg	45.25%
Niacin 2.757mg	17.23%
Riboflavin 0.434mg	33.38%
Thiamin 0.442mg	36.83%
Vitamin B-12 0µg	
Vitamin B-6 0.721mg	55.46%
Vitamin D 0IU	
Vitamin E 1.26mg	8.40%

Vitamin K 1379.1µg	**1149.25%**

Minerals

Copper 2.146mg	**238.44%**
Magnesium 139mg	**33.10%**
Phosphorus 251mg	**35.86%**
Selenium 3µg	**5.45%**
Zinc 1.73mg	**15.73%**

Other

Caffeine 0mg
Theobromine 0mg
Water 784.86g

All nutrient values are calculated from the USDA nutrition database.

Apple Cucumber Spinach

Over-the-top in Vitamin K, and high in copper and Vitamin C.

Yields 1 glass.

Ingredients

- 2 medium apples, cored
- 1 cucumber
- 4 leaves kale
- 1 lemon
- 2 cups spinach

Directions

1. Wash the fruits and vegetables thoroughly.
2. Put all the ingredients into a juicer and process them.
3. Shake or stir.
4. Serve immediately.

Nutrition Facts (Juiced)

Calories 200
Calories from Fat 16.76

	% Daily Value *
Total Fat 1.86g	5.31%
Saturated Fat 0.281g	1.41%
Monounsaturated Fat 0.088g	
Polyunsaturated Fat 0.634g	
Cholesterol 0mg	

Sodium 78mg	**5.20%**
Potassium 1354mg	**28.81%**
Total Carbohydrate 56.27g	**43.63%**
Dietary Fiber 1.3g	**3.42%**
Sugars 31.1g	
Protein 7.87	
Vitamin A 706µg	**78.44%**
Vitamin C 168.5mg	**187.22%**
Calcium 248mg	**24.80%**
Iron 4.9mg	**46.50%**

* The Percent Daily Values are based on a 2,000 calorie diet, so your values may change depending on your calorie needs. The values here may not be 100% accurate because the recipes have not been professionally evaluated nor have they been evaluated by the U.S. FDA.

Vitamins

Choline 31.5mg	**5.73%**
Folate 139µg	**34.75%**
Niacin 1.763mg	**11.02%**
Riboflavin 0.351mg	**27.00%**
Thiamin 0.257mg	**21.42%**
Vitamin B-12 0µg	
Vitamin B-6 0.569mg	**43.77%**
Vitamin D 0IU	
Vitamin E 1.44mg	**9.60%**
Vitamin K 933.7µg	**778.08%**

Minerals

Copper 1.694mg	**188.22%**
Magnesium 123mg	**29.29%**
Phosphorus 196mg	**28.00%**
Selenium 2.1µg	**3.82%**
Zinc 1.32mg	**12.00%**
Other	
Caffeine 0mg	
Theobromine 0mg	
Water 575.53g	

All nutrient values are calculated from the USDA nutrition database.

Celery Carrot Cucumber Cocktail

Fairly sweet, even though it's loaded with healthy vegies.

Yields 2 glasses (32 oz.).

Ingredients

- 2 medium apples, cored
- 1 beet
- 4 medium carrots
- 3 large stalks celery
- ½ cucumber
- ½ thumb ginger root

Directions

1. Wash the fruits and vegetables thoroughly.
2. Put all the ingredients into a juicer and process them.
3. Shake or stir.
4. Serve immediately.

Nutrition Facts (Juiced)

Calories 237
Calories from Fat 16.76

	% Daily Value *
Total Fat 1.46g	4.17%
Saturated Fat 0.28g	1.40%
Monounsaturated Fat 0.142g	
Polyunsaturated Fat 0.556g	

Cholesterol 0mg

Sodium 327mg	**21.80%**
Potassium 1756mg	**37.36%**
Total Carbohydrate 72.57g	**55.82%**
Dietary Fiber 2.5g	**6.58%**
Sugars 47.21g	
Protein 5.99	
Vitamin A 1471µg	**163.44%**
Vitamin C 35.3mg	**39.22%**
Calcium 163mg	**16.30%**
Iron 2.41mg	**30.12%**

* The Percent Daily Values are based on a 2,000 calorie diet, so your values may change depending on your calorie needs. The values here may not be 100% accurate because the recipes have not been professionally evaluated nor have they been evaluated by the U.S. FDA.

Vitamins

Choline 48mg	**8.73%**
Folate 230µg	**57.50%**
Niacin 2.916mg	**18.22%**
Riboflavin 0.329mg	**25.31%**
Thiamin 0.253mg	**21.08%**
Vitamin B-12 0µg	
Vitamin B-6 0.577mg	**44.38%**
Vitamin D 0IU	
Vitamin E 2.05mg	**13.67%**
Vitamin K 85.1µg	**70.92%**

Minerals

Copper 0.347mg	**38.56%**
Magnesium 94mg	**22.38%**
Phosphorus 197mg	**28.14%**
Selenium 1.9μg	**3.45%**
Zinc 1.35mg	**12.27%**

Other

Caffeine 0mg	
Theobromine 0mg	
Water 711.3g	

All nutrient values are calculated from the USDA nutrition database.

Red Tangy Spice

With all the cool drinks we've offered you, we had to end with a hot one.

Yields 1 glass.

Ingredients

- 1 beet
- 3 large carrots, topped
- 2 large stalks celery
- 1 thumb ginger root
- ½ lime
- 1 jalapeno pepper
- 2 cups spinach

Directions

1. Wash the fruits and vegetables thoroughly.
2. Put all the ingredients into a juicer and process them.
3. Shake or stir.
4. Serve immediately.

Nutrition Facts (Juiced)

Calories 121
Calories from Fat 9.87

	% Daily Value *
Total Fat 1.1g	**3.14%**
Saturated Fat 0.201g	**1.00%**

Monounsaturated Fat 0.126g	
Polyunsaturated Fat 0.44g	
Cholesterol 0mg	
Sodium 308mg	**20.53%**
Potassium 1467mg	**31.21%**
Total Carbohydrate 36.48g	**28.06%**
Dietary Fiber 1.6g	**4.21%**
Sugars 18.35g	
Protein 5.76g	
Vitamin A 1487µg	**165.22%**
Vitamin C 48.8mg	**54.22%**
Calcium 159mg	**15.90%**
Iron 3.02mg	**37.75%**

* The Percent Daily Values are based on a 2,000 calorie diet, so your values may change depending on your calorie needs. The values here may not be 100% accurate because the recipes have not been professionally evaluated nor have they been evaluated by the U.S. FDA.

Vitamins	
Choline 41mg	**7.45%**
Folate 282µg	**70.50%**
Niacin 2.785mg	**17.41%**
Riboflavin 0.284mg	**21.85%**
Thiamin 0.204mg	**17.00%**
Vitamin B-12 0µg	
Vitamin B-6 0.517mg	**39.77%**
Vitamin D 0IU	

Vitamin E 2.59mg	**17.27%**
Vitamin K 251.2µg	**209.33%**
Minerals	
Copper 0.304mg	**33.78%**
Magnesium 99mg	**23.57%**
Phosphorus 156mg	**22.29%**
Selenium 2µg	**3.64%**
Zinc 1.23mg	**11.18%**
Other	
Caffeine 0mg	
Theobromine 0mg	
Water 407.61g	
All nutrient values are calculated from the USDA nutrition database.	

Conclusion

Thank you again for downloading this book.

I hope the delicious recipes in this book helped you in planning your nutritional program. Unlike many juicing books, we've presented a complete nutritional analysis for almost every recipe, as well as adding other helpful information for dieters and health-conscious readers.

In this book, we've presented recipes in organized sections that help you find the type of recipe you're looking for. We hope we've made it easier to chart a path of better nutrition. We hope your next step is to stick with your nutritional program so that you can continue to lose weight and gain health.

Good luck!

Helpful Resources

http://www.juicingforweightloss.com/juicing-recipes

http://www.healthy-juicing.com/juicing-recipes/

http://allrecipes.com/recipes/drinks/juice/

http://juicerecipes.com/

http://blog.williams-sonoma.com/30-days-of-juicing/

http://www.rebootwithjoe.com/

http://foodbabe.com/2013/08/05/juicing-mistakes/

http://www.all-about-juicing.com/Fruit_Juice_Recipes.html

Juicy Drinks by Valerie Aikman-Smith

Juicer Cookbook by Carol Gelles (Williams-Sonoma Cookware Series)

Breville Health Full Life by Breville USA

Preview of Gluten Free Diet Guide: A Blueprint to Jump Starting a Healthy, Low Budget, Gluten-Free Diet

Background

Gluten is a protein compound present in cereal grains such as wheat, rye and barley. Gluten is a Latin word which translates to "glue," referring to the combined water-insoluble proteins, gliadin and glutenin. Gluten is the substance that makes dough elastic and processed food items like bread, pasta and pastries chewy. This substance may also be present in cosmetics such as make-up and hair products.

A significant percentage of the population in North America have sensitivity to gluten where they experience an elevated immunologic response when they ingest foods that contain gluten. This usually leads to symptoms such as joint pain, anemia, tiredness, infertility, neurological disorders, dermatitis, and celiac disease, an autoimmune disorder.

The only known treatment for these health issues is to totally embrace a gluten-free diet. This means the person has to steer clear of foods that contain rye, barley, wheat, and other associated cereal grains. Because of the popularity of these grains in the food market, it is possible that items claiming to be gluten-free may have minute amounts of wheat, rye, or barley that is substantial enough to cause symptoms to persons that are sensitive to gluten.

Symptoms and disorders caused by gluten-containing food items

A review from the New England Journal of Medicine came up with a listing of illnesses caused by ingestion of gluten. Symptoms include Attention Deficit Hyperactivity Disorder (ADHD), anxiety, arthritis, depression, Irritable Bowel Syndrome (IBS), recurrent headaches, osteoporosis, eczema, fatigue, uncoordinated muscles, compromised immune system, inflammation of organs, excessive growth of fungus, weight loss or weight gain, and deficient nutrition. People who are hypersensitive to gluten are at high risk to develop diabetes, Gastro-Intestinal cancers, obesity, brain disorders, thyroid problems, and autism.

Costs involved with a gluten-free diet

A recent study assessed the economic burden of subscribing to a total gluten-free diet. The researchers conducted an analysis of food products that use wheat classified by brand name, size or weight of the package, and evaluated them in contrast to items that are gluten-free. The price disparities were also evaluated among different store venues like general stores, more expensive grocery stores, health food stores, and online grocery sites.

The study found that availability of gluten-free products varies among stores. General grocery stores offer 36 percent, while upper class grocery stores have 41 percent, and health food stores carry 94 percent in comparison to a hundred percent availability in online grocery sites. On the whole, all gluten-free products were costlier than wheat-based food items. Gluten-free pasta and bread are double the price of wheat-based pastas and breads.

Apparently, the purchase venue had more impact on the price ranges than geographic location. Researchers conclude that gluten-free items are not as available and are costlier than products that contain gluten. The author emphasizes that there is a need to address availability and cost issues of gluten-free foods that affect the dietary adherence and quality of life of gluten-sensitive consumers.

To fully enjoy this book, visit: http://www.amazon.com/Gluten-Free-Diet-Guide-Blueprint-ebook/dp/B00I135OZO

Did You Like This Book?

Before you leave, I wanted to say thank you again for buying my book.

I know you could have picked from a number of different books on this topic, but you chose this one so I can't thank you enough for doing that and reading until the end.

I'd like to ask you a small favor.

If you enjoyed this book or feel that it has helped you in anyway, then could you please take a minute and post an honest review about it on Amazon?

Click here to post a review.

Your review will help get my book out there to more people and they'll be grateful, as will I.

More Books You Might Like

Household DIY: Save Time and Money with Do It Yourself Hints and Tips on Furniture, Clothes, Pests, Stains, Residues, Odors and More!

DIY Household Hacks: Save Time and Money with Do It Yourself Tips and Tricks for Cleaning Your House

Essential Oils: Essential Oils & Aromatherapy for Beginners: Proven Secrets to Weight Loss, Skin Care, Hair Care & Stress Relief Using Essential Oil Recipes

Apple Cider Vinegar for Beginners: An Apple Cider Vinegar Handbook with Proven Secrets to Natural Weight Loss, Optimum Health and Beautiful Skin

Body Butter Recipes: Proven Formula Secrets to Making All Natural Body Butters that Will Hydrate and Rejuvenate Your Skin

If the links do not work, for whatever reason, you can simply search for these titles on the Amazon website to find them.

CPSIA information can be obtained at www.ICGtesting.com
Printed in the USA
LVOW07s1224061215

465619LV00025B/2973/P

9 781511 449434